(ex·ploring) SERIES

1. Investigating in a systematic way: examining. 2. Searching
into or ranging over for the purpose of discovery.

Getting Started with

Microsoft®
OneNote® 2016

Series Editor Mary Anne Poatsy

Linda Pogue

Series Created by Dr. Robert T. Grauer

Pearson

330 Hudson Street, NY, NY 10013

Vice President of IT & Career Skills: Andrew Gilfillan

Senior Portfolio Manager: Samantha Lewis

Team Lead, Project Management: Laura Burgess

Project Manager: Barbara Stover

Development Editor: Barbara Stover

Editorial Assistant: Michael Campbell

Director of Product Marketing: Maggie Waples

Director of Field Marketing: Leigh Ann Sims

Product Marketing Manager: Kaylee Carlson

Field Marketing Managers: Molly Schmidt & Joanna Conley

Senior Operations Specialist: Maura Zaldivar-Garcia

Interior and Cover Design: Cenveo

Senior Product Model Manager: Eric Hakanson

Production and Digital Studio Lead: Heather Darby

Course Producer, MyITLab: Amanda Losonsky

Digital Project Manager, MyITLab: Becca Lowe

Media Project Manager, Production: John Cassar

Full-Service Project Management: Amy Kopperude, iEnergizer Aptara®, Ltd.

Composition: iEnergizer Aptara®, Ltd.

Cover Image Credits: cunico/Fotolia (*compass rose*); mawrhis/Fotolia (*checker pattern*); wavebreakmedia/Shutterstock (*students*); Sergey Nivens/Fotolia(*world*); dotshock/Shutterstock (*business people*)

Library of Congress Control Number on File

1 16

ISBN 10:   0-13-449710-4

ISBN 13: 978-0-13-449710-5

About the Author

Mary Anne Poatsy, Series Editor, Computing Concepts Author

Mary Anne is a senior faculty member at Montgomery County Community College, teaching various computer application and concepts courses in face-to-face and online environments. She holds a B.A. in Psychology and Education from Mount Holyoke College and an M.B.A. in Finance from Northwestern University's Kellogg Graduate School of Management.

Mary Anne has more than 18 years of educational experience. She is currently adjunct faculty at Montgomery County Community College. She has also taught at Gywnedd Mercy University, Bucks County Community College, and Muhlenberg College, as well as conducted personal training. Before teaching, she was Vice President at Shearson Lehman in the Municipal Bond Investment Banking Department.

Linda Pogue

Linda Pogue graduated magna cum laude from the University of Arkansas at Monticello in 2001 with a B.S. in Computer Information Systems and was awarded Information Systems Division Outstanding Senior of 2001. She earned an M.S. in Computer Information Systems from the University of Phoenix in 2003, and an M.S. in Education with an emphasis in Instructional Design for Online Learning from Capella University in 2009. After working as a computer programmer, she moved into the field of education. She has taught computer information courses at her alma mater—University of Arkansas at Monticello–as well as at Northwest Arkansas Community College and Bryan College (now Bryan University). After seven years of teaching, Linda decided in 2011 to go full time into authoring and technical editing of college-level supplements and textbooks.

Dedications

For my husband, Ted, who unselfishly continues to take on more than his share to support me throughout the process; and for my children, Laura, Carolyn, and Teddy, whose encouragement and love have been inspiring.

Mary Anne Poatsy

For Charles, who worries about me when I don't get out of my chair often enough, brings me coffee while I work, and loves me unconditionally. To Larry and Susan–may your future be bright. To Scott and Sandra–may your dreams be fulfilled. To all my sweet grandchildren–Charles, Naomi, Ariana, Elizabeth, Melody, and Jesse–thank you all for all you do.

Linda Pogue

Contents

OneNote 2016

Acknowledgments

The Exploring team acknowledges and thanks all the reviewers who helped us throughout the years by providing us with their invaluable comments, suggestions, and constructive criticism.

Adriana Lumpkin
Midland College

Alan S. Abrahams
Virginia Tech

Alexandre C. Probst
Colorado Christian University

Ali Berrached
University of Houston–Downtown

Allen Alexander
Delaware Technical & Community College

Andrea Marchese
Maritime College, State University of New York

Andrew Blitz
Broward College; Edison State College

Angel Norman
University of Tennessee, Knoxville

Angela Clark
University of South Alabama

Ann Rovetto
Horry-Georgetown Technical College

Astrid Todd
Guilford Technical Community College

Audrey Gillant
Maritime College, State University of New York

Barbara Stover
Marion Technical College

Barbara Tollinger
Sinclair Community College

Ben Brahim Taha
Auburn University

Beverly Amer
Northern Arizona University

Beverly Fite
Amarillo College

Biswadip Ghosh
Metropolitan State University of Denver

Bonita Volker
Tidewater Community College

Bonnie Homan
San Francisco State University

Brad West
Sinclair Community College

Brian Powell
West Virginia University

Carol Buser
Owens Community College

Carol Roberts
University of Maine

Carolyn Barren
Macomb Community College

Carolyn Borne
Louisiana State University

Cathy Poyner
Truman State University

Charles Hodgson
Delgado Community College

Chen Zhang
Bryant University

Cheri Higgins
Illinois State University

Cheryl Brown
Delgado Community College

Cheryl Hinds
Norfolk State University

Cheryl Sypniewski
Macomb Community College

Chris Robinson
Northwest State Community College

Cindy Herbert
Metropolitan Community College–Longview

Craig J. Peterson
American InterContinental University

Dana Hooper
University of Alabama

Dana Johnson
North Dakota State University

Daniela Marghitu
Auburn University

David Noel
University of Central Oklahoma

David Pulis
Maritime College, State University of New York

David Thornton
Jacksonville State University

Dawn Medlin
Appalachian State University

Debby Keen
University of Kentucky

Debra Chapman
University of South Alabama

Debra Hoffman
Southeast Missouri State University

Derrick Huang
Florida Atlantic University

Diana Baran
Henry Ford Community College

Diane Cassidy
The University of North Carolina at Charlotte

Diane L. Smith
Henry Ford Community College

Dick Hewer
Ferris State College

Don Danner
San Francisco State University

Don Hoggan
Solano College

Don Riggs
SUNY Schenectady County Community College

Doncho Petkov
Eastern Connecticut State University

Donna Ehrhart
State University of New York at Brockport

Elaine Crable
Xavier University

Elizabeth Duett
Delgado Community College

Erhan Uskup
Houston Community College–Northwest

Eric Martin
University of Tennessee

Erika Nadas
Wilbur Wright College

Floyd Winters
Manatee Community College

Frank Lucente
Westmoreland County Community College

G. Jan Wilms
Union University

Gail Cope
Sinclair Community College

Gary DeLorenzo
California University of Pennsylvania

Gary Garrison
Belmont University

Gary McFall
Purdue University

George Cassidy
Sussex County Community College

Gerald Braun
Xavier University

Gerald Burgess
Western New Mexico University

Gladys Swindler
Fort Hays State University

Hector Frausto
California State University Los Angeles

Heith Hennel
Valencia Community College

Henry Rudzinski
Central Connecticut State University

Irene Joos
La Roche College

Iwona Rusin
Baker College; Davenport University

J. Roberto Guzman
San Diego Mesa College

Jacqueline D. Lawson
Henry Ford Community College

Jakie Brown Jr.
Stevenson University

James Brown
Central Washington University

James Powers
University of Southern Indiana

Jane Stam
Onondaga Community College

Janet Bringhurst
Utah State University

Jean Welsh
Lansing Community College

Jeanette Dix
Ivy Tech Community College

Jennifer Day
Sinclair Community College

Jill Canine
Ivy Tech Community College

Jill Young
Southeast Missouri State University

Jim Chaffee
The University of Iowa Tippie College
of Business

Joanne Lazirko
University of Wisconsin–Milwaukee

Jodi Milliner
Kansas State University

John Hollenbeck
Blue Ridge Community College

John Seydel
Arkansas State University

Judith A. Scheeren
Westmoreland County Community College

Judith Brown
The University of Memphis

Juliana Cypert
Tarrant County College

Kamaljeet Sanghera
George Mason University

Karen Priestly
Northern Virginia Community College

Karen Ravan
Spartanburg Community College

Karen Tracey
Central Connecticut State University

Kathleen Brenan
Ashland University

Ken Busbee
Houston Community College

Kent Foster
Winthrop University

Kevin Anderson
Solano Community College

Kim Wright
The University of Alabama

Kristen Hockman
University of Missouri–Columbia

Kristi Smith
Allegany College of Maryland

Laura Marcoulides
Fullerton College

Laura McManamon
University of Dayton

Laurence Boxer
Niagara University

Leanne Chun
Leeward Community College

Lee McClain
Western Washington University

Linda D. Collins
Mesa Community College

Linda Johnsonius
Murray State University

Linda Lau
Longwood University

Linda Theus
Jackson State Community College

Linda Williams
Marion Technical College

Lisa Miller
University of Central Oklahoma

Lister Horn
Pensacola Junior College

Lixin Tao
Pace University

Loraine Miller
Cayuga Community College

Lori Kielty
Central Florida Community College

Lorna Wells
Salt Lake Community College

Lorraine Sauchin
Duquesne University

Lucy Parakhovnik
California State University, Northridge

Lynn Keane
University of South Carolina

Lynn Mancini
Delaware Technical Community College

Mackinzee Escamilla
South Plains College

Marcia Welch
Highline Community College

Margaret McManus
Northwest Florida State College

Margaret Warrick
Allan Hancock College

Marilyn Hibbert
Salt Lake Community College

Mark Choman
Luzerne County Community College

Maryann Clark
University of New Hampshire

Mary Beth Tarver
Northwestern State University

Mary Duncan
University of Missouri–St. Louis

Melissa Nemeth
Indiana University-Purdue University
Indianapolis

Melody Alexander
Ball State University

Michael Douglas
University of Arkansas at Little Rock

Michael Dunklebarger
Alamance Community College

Michael G. Skaff
College of the Sequoias

Michele Budnovitch
Pennsylvania College of Technology

Mike Jochen
East Stroudsburg University

Mike Michaelson
Palomar College

Mike Scroggins
Missouri State University

Mimi Spain
Southern Maine Community College

Muhammed Badamas
Morgan State University

NaLisa Brown
University of the Ozarks

Nancy Grant
Community College of Allegheny
County–South Campus

Nanette Lareau
University of Arkansas Community
College–Morrilton

Nikia Robinson
Indian River State University

Pam Brune
Chattanooga State Community College

Pam Uhlenkamp
Iowa Central Community College

Patrick Smith
Marshall Community and Technical College

Paul Addison
Ivy Tech Community College

Paula Ruby
Arkansas State University

Peggy Burrus
Red Rocks Community College

Peter Ross
SUNY Albany

Philip H. Nielson
Salt Lake Community College

Philip Valvalides
Guilford Technical Community College

Ralph Hooper
University of Alabama

Ranette Halverson
Midwestern State University

Richard Blamer
John Carroll University

Richard Cacace
Pensacola Junior College

Richard Hewer
Ferris State University

Richard Sellers
Hill College

Rob Murray
Ivy Tech Community College

Robert Banta
Macomb Community College

Robert Dušek
Northern Virginia Community College

Robert G. Phipps Jr.
West Virginia University

Robert Sindt
Johnson County Community College

Robert Warren
Delgado Community College

Rocky Belcher
Sinclair Community College

Roger Pick
University of Missouri at Kansas City

Ronnie Creel
Troy University

Rosalie Westerberg
Clover Park Technical College

Ruth Neal
Navarro College

Sandra Thomas
Troy University

Sheila Gionfriddo
Luzerne County Community College

Sherrie Geitgey
Northwest State Community College

Sherry Lenhart
Terra Community College

Sophia Wilberscheid
Indian River State College

Sophie Lee
California State University, Long Beach

Stacy Johnson
Iowa Central Community College

Stephanie Kramer
Northwest State Community College

Stephen Z. Jourdan
Auburn University at Montgomery

Steven Schwarz
Raritan Valley Community College

Sue A. McCrory
Missouri State University

Sumathy Chandrashekar
Salisbury University

Susan Fuschetto
Cerritos College

Susan Medlin
UNC Charlotte

Susan N. Dozier
Tidewater Community College

Suzan Spitzberg
Oakton Community College

Suzanne M. Jeska
County College of Morris

Sven Aelterman
Troy University

Sy Hirsch
Sacred Heart University

Sylvia Brown
Midland College

Tanya Patrick
Clackamas Community College

Terri Holly
Indian River State College

Terry Ray Rigsby
Hill College

Thomas Rienzo
Western Michigan University

Tina Johnson
Midwestern State University

Tommy Lu
Delaware Technical Community College

Troy S. Cash
Northwest Arkansas Community College

Vicki Robertson
Southwest Tennessee Community

Vickie Pickett
Midland College

Weifeng Chen
California University of Pennsylvania

Wes Anthony
Houston Community College

William Ayen
University of Colorado at Colorado Springs

Wilma Andrews
Virginia Commonwealth University

Yvonne Galusha
University of Iowa

Special thanks to our content development and technical team:

Barbara Stover

Sharon Behrens

Julie Boyles

Joyce Nielsen

Preface

The Exploring Series and You

Exploring is Pearson's Office Application series that requires students like you to think "beyond the point and click." In this edition, we have worked to restructure the Exploring experience around the way you, today's modern student, actually use your resources.

The goal of Exploring is, as it has always been, to go farther than teaching just the steps to accomplish a task—the series provides the theoretical foundation for you to understand when and why to apply a skill. As a result, you achieve a deeper understanding of each application and can apply this critical thinking beyond Office and the classroom.

The How & Why of This Revision

Outcomes matter. Whether it's getting a good grade in this course, learning how to use Microsoft Office and Windows 10 so students can be successful in other courses, or learning a specific skill that will make learners successful in a future job, everyone has an outcome in mind. And outcomes matter. That is why we revised our chapter opener to focus on the outcomes students will achieve by working through each Exploring chapter. These are coupled with objectives and skills, providing a map students can follow to get everything they need from each chapter.

Critical Thinking and Collaboration are essential 21st-century skills. Students want and need to be successful in their future careers—so we use motivating case studies to show relevance of these skills to future careers.

Students today read, prepare, and study differently than students used to. Students use textbooks like a tool—they want to easily identify what they need to know and learn it efficiently. We have added key features, such as Tasks Lists (in purple) and Step Icons, and tracked everything via page numbers that allow efficient navigation, creating a map students can easily follow.

Students are exposed to technology. The new edition of Exploring moves beyond the basics of the software at a faster pace, without sacrificing coverage of the fundamental skills that students need to know.

Students are diverse. Students can be any age, any gender, any race, with any level of ability or learning style. With this in mind, we broadened our definition of "student resources" to include MyITLab, the most powerful and most ADA-compliant online homework and assessment tool around with a direct 1:1 content match with the Exploring Series. Exploring will be accessible to all students, regardless of learning style.

Providing You with a Map to Success to Move Beyond the Point and Click

All of these changes and additions will provide students an easy and efficient path to follow to be successful in this course, regardless of where they start at the beginning of this course. Our goal is to keep students engaged in both the hands-on and conceptual sides, helping achieve a higher level of understanding that will guarantee success in this course and in a future career.

In addition to the vision and experience of the series creator, Robert T. Grauer, we have assembled a tremendously talented team of Office Applications authors who have devoted themselves to teaching the ins and outs of Microsoft Word, Excel, Access, and PowerPoint. Led in this edition by series editor Mary Anne Poatsy, the whole team is dedicated to the Exploring mission of moving students **beyond the point and click**.

Key Features

The **How/Why Approach** helps students move beyond the point and click to a true understanding of how to apply Microsoft Office skills.

- **White Pages/Yellow Pages** clearly distinguish the theory (white pages) from the skills covered in the Hands-On Exercises (yellow pages) so students always know what they are supposed to be doing and why.

- **Case Study** presents a scenario for the chapter, creating a story that ties the Hands-On Exercises together.

The **Outcomes focus** allows students and instructors to know the higher-level learning goals and how those are achieved through discreet objectives and skills.

- **Outcomes** presented at the beginning of each chapter identify the learning goals for students and instructors.

- **Enhanced Objective Mapping** enables students to follow a directed path through each chapter, from the objectives list at the chapter opener through the exercises at the end of the chapter.
  - **Objectives List:** This provides a simple list of key objectives covered in the chapter. This includes page numbers so students can skip between objectives where they feel they need the most help.
  - **Step Icons:** These icons appear in the white pages and reference the step numbers in the Hands-On Exercises, providing a correlation between the two so students can easily find conceptual help when they are working hands-on and need a refresher.
  - **Quick Concepts Check:** A series of questions that appear briefly at the end of each white page section. These questions cover the most essential concepts in the white pages required for students to be successful in working the Hands-On Exercises. Page numbers are included for easy reference to help students locate the answers.
  - **Chapter Objectives Review:** Appears toward the end of the chapter and reviews all important concepts throughout the chapter. Newly designed in an easy-to-read bulleted format.

End-of-Chapter Exercises offer instructors several options for assessment. Each chapter has exercises ranging from multiple-choice questions to open-ended projects.

- **Multiple Choice, Key Terms Matching, Practice Exercises, Mid-Level Exercises, Beyond the Classroom Exercises, and Capstone Exercises** appear at the end of all chapters.

Resources

Instructor Resources

The Instructor's Resource Center, available at **www.pearsonhighered.com**, includes the -following:

- **Instructor Manual** provides one-stop-shop for instructors, including an overview of all available resources, teaching tips, as well as student data and solution files for every exercise.

- **Solution Files with Scorecards** assist with grading the Hands-On Exercises and end-of-chapter exercises.

- **Prepared Exams** allow instructors to assess all skills covered in a chapter with a single project.

- **Rubrics** for Mid-Level Creative Cases and Beyond the Classroom Cases in Microsoft Word format enable instructors to customize the assignments for their classes.

- **PowerPoint Presentations** with notes for each chapter are included for out-of-class study or review.

- **Multiple Choice, Key Term Matching, and Quick Concepts Check Answer Keys**

- **Test Bank** provides objective-based questions for every chapter.

- **Scripted Lectures** offer an in-class lecture guide for instructors to mirror the Hands-On Exercises.

- **Syllabus Templates**
  - Outcomes, Objectives, and Skills List
  - Assignment Sheet
  - File Guide

Student Resources

Student Data Files

Access your student data files needed to complete the exercises in this textbook at **www.pearsonhighered.com/exploring**.

Available in MyITLab

- **Multiple Choice quizzes** enable you to test concepts you have learned by answering auto-graded questions.

- **eText** available in some MyITLab courses and includes links to videos, student data files, and other learning aids.

Getting Started with

Microsoft® OneNote® 2016

Getting Started with OneNote 2016

LEARNING OUTCOMES

- You will create a new notebook and add sections and pages.
- You will add photos, documents, screenshots, and other files to the notebook pages.

OBJECTIVES AND SKILLS: After you read this chapter, you will be able to:

CASE STUDY | Pearson University Majors

Bonnie Duckett is an undergraduate student majoring in Information Systems Management in the College of Technology & Computing at Pearson University, a prestigious university on the East Coast. Last semester, Bonnie lost an important spiral notebook containing study notes for her Basic Programming class, which put her in a panic when it was time to study for final exams.

This semester her Systems Analysis and Design Methods instructor, Dr. Vamil Singh, has recommended that she use OneNote to track course and lecture notes, appointments, and assignments. Bonnie is excited about the various possibilities for taking and keeping track of her notes, and wants to learn more about the application.

CHAPTER 1

Creating, Managing, and Integrating OneNote Notebooks

YakobchukOlena/Fotolia

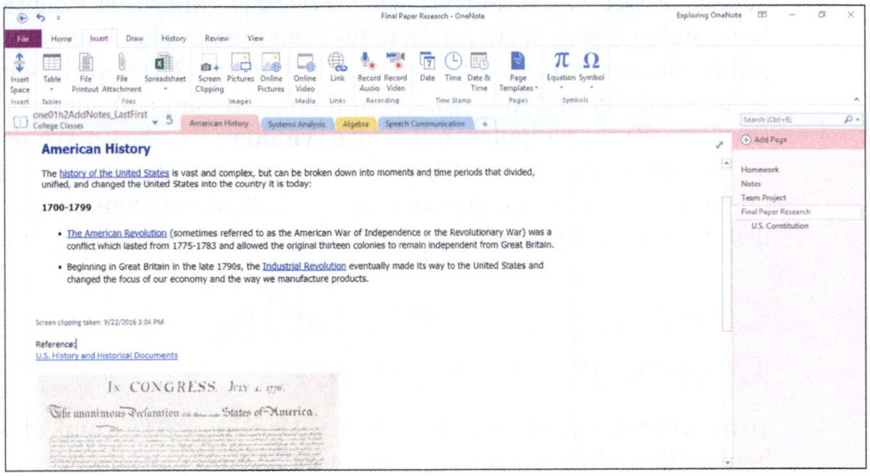

OneNote 2016, Windows 10, Microsoft Corporation

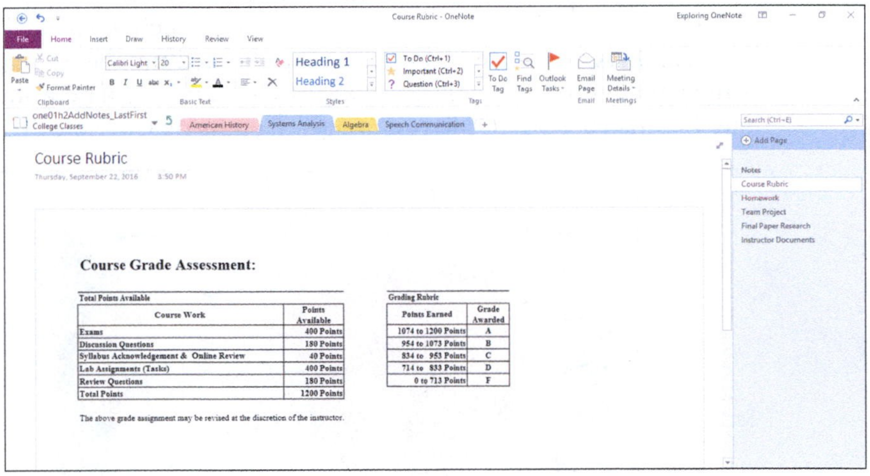

OneNote 2016, Windows 10, Microsoft Corporation

FIGURE 1.1 Pearson University Majors Notebook

CASE STUDY | Pearson University Majors

Starting Files	Files to be Submitted
Blank notebook	one01h1Jon_LastFirst.onepkg
one01h2Development.jpg	one01h1ClassNotes_LastFirst.onepkg
one01h2Linking.docx	one01h2AddNotes_LastFirst.onepkg
one01h2Rubric.xlsx	
one01h2Schedule.xlsx	
one01h2Tech.docx	
one01h2Template.potx	
one01h2Whiteboard.jpg	

Introduction to OneNote 2016

Notes in one form or another are a part of our lives. Whether they are used to remind us of important dates, to pick up our dry cleaning, or how to complete a specific task on the computer, notes help keep us on track. With the invention of Post-it Notes, 3M's handy stick up notes, many of us now work in paper studded office areas and homes. If the note you need at school is stuck above your desk in your room, you don't have access to it when you're studying in the library.

OneNote is a note-taking software application used by students, office assistants, managers, and professionals to keep track of important information and tasks. With the advent of web-based software, **OneNote 2016**, Microsoft's digital note-taking application, makes it possible to access notes from home, school, office, or any location or computing device that has Internet access. OneNote 2016 works with desktop computers, laptops, tablets, and Android, iOS, and Windows smartphones. For the desktop version of OneNote 2016, computers must have Windows 7 or newer Windows operating systems.

In this section, you will learn how to create and manage OneNote 2016 notebooks on your desktop or laptop computer. You will add sections and pages, rename and organize sections and pages, and print and export sections and pages.

Creating and Managing OneNote Notebooks

To better understand the concept behind OneNote 2016, think of the familiar spiral notebook with multiple tabbed sections for different topics (see Figure 1.2). Within each section, there are multiple pages of content. Unlike a spiral notebook with its fixed capacity, OneNote has an unlimited number of notebooks. Each **notebook** has an unlimited number of **sections**, and each section has an unlimited number of **pages** (see Figure 1.3). If a single notebook becomes large enough to be unwieldy, a new one can be created at any time. The instructions in this text are based on using OneNote 2016 in Windows 10.

Sections

Pages

Colorlife/Fotolia

FIGURE 1.2 Spiral Notebook with Sections and Pages

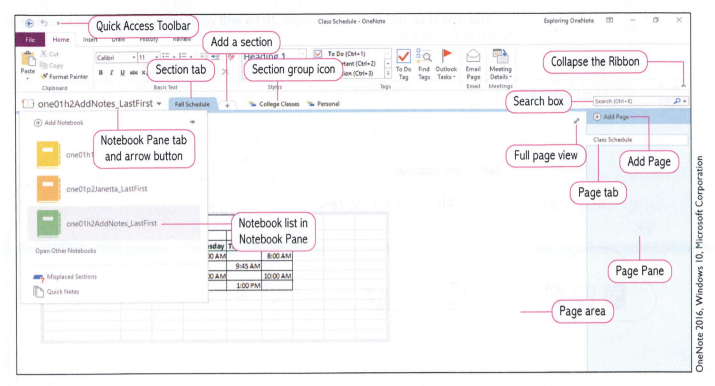

FIGURE 1.3 OneNote 2016 Notebook

To open OneNote 2016 in Windows 10, click the Start button in the bottom left corner of your screen. If the OneNote 2016 tile is not on the Start menu, scroll through the Apps pane until you find OneNote 2016, and click the application name. To add the application tile to the Start menu, right-click on OneNote 2016, and then click Pin to Start. To add the icon for OneNote 2016 to the taskbar, right-click on OneNote 2016, point to More, and then click Pin to taskbar.

> **TIP: ONENOTE 2016 VS. ONENOTE**
> You may notice two OneNote listings in the Apps pane, OneNote 2016 and OneNote. OneNote 2016 is the full version of OneNote, while OneNote is a limited, free version of the application installed by default in the Windows 10 operating system. For this chapter, be sure you select the OneNote 2016 application rather than OneNote in the Apps pane. OneNote will be used in Chapter 2. If for some reason you do not have the OneNote app on your computer, it is available for download from the Microsoft Store.

The first time you sign in, OneNote 2016 will open with a Quick Notes section as shown in Figure 1.4.

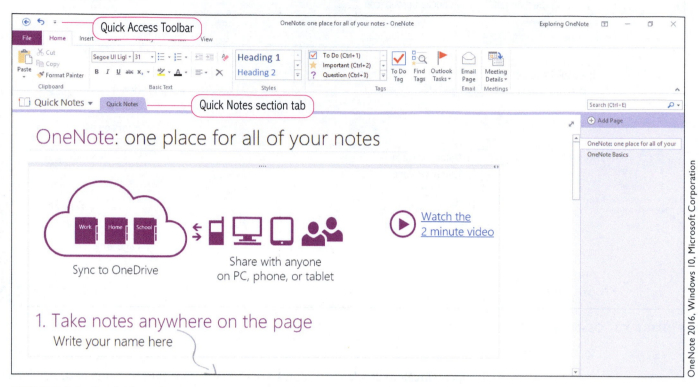

FIGURE 1.4 Quick Notes Section

> **TIP: IF YOU DO NOT HAVE A MICROSOFT ACCOUNT**
> If you do not have a Microsoft account, OneNote will open with a blank section containing a blank page. Some features, such as syncing your notebook to OneDrive, will require you to create a Microsoft account. Syncing the notebook to OneDrive mirrors the notebook on the cloud, so that all your Internet-connected devices can access the same content. A Microsoft account can be created through www.onedrive.live.com.

The first time you open OneNote 2016, the application creates a new notebook named *My Notebook*. If OneNote 2016 has been previously opened, the notebook that was open when you closed the application will open. If no notebooks were open when the application was previously closed, you will see the following message: *You don't have any open notebooks* (see Figure 1.5).

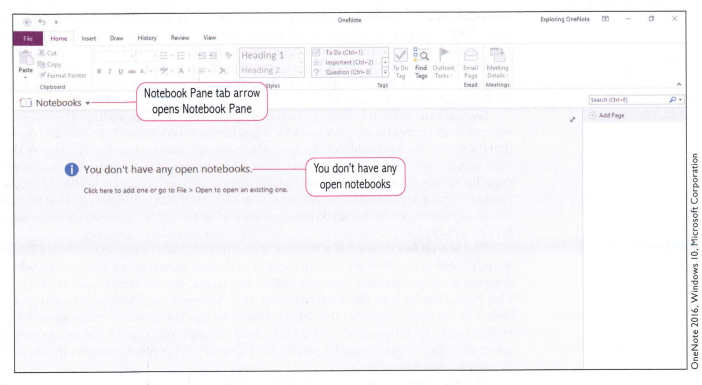

FIGURE 1.5 No Open Notebooks Message

Discover the OneNote 2016 Interface

At the top left corner of the window, the **Quick Access Toolbar** in OneNote 2016 contains three command buttons: Back, Undo, and Customize Quick Access Toolbar. Systems with a touch screen may also have the Touch/Mouse Mode button in the Quick Access Toolbar. The OneNote 2016 interface features a **Ribbon** that contains tabs. Each tab contains groups of commands that enable you to manage, manipulate, and format your OneNote 2016 page contents. Contextual tabs are tabs that only display when you are working with specific items such as tables, equations, or audio or video recordings. For instance, when a table is inserted on a page, while the table is still selected, the contextual Table Tools Layout tab displays.

The Ribbon can be collapsed to give more room for the page area. To collapse the Ribbon, click the Collapse the Ribbon button above the right end of the Search box (see Figure 1.6). The Ribbon is also expanded or collapsed by double-clicking a tab. The

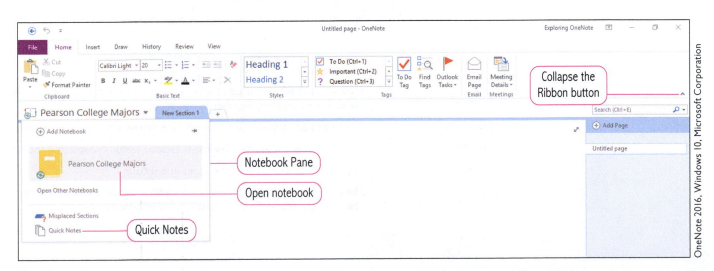

FIGURE 1.6 Notebook Pane

Notebook Pane is minimized by default. It is used to access other OneNote notebooks, add a notebook, open notebooks not listed, review misplaced sections, or open **Quick Notes**. The Quick Notes section contains pages with notes that have not yet been moved to a notebook. Display the Notebook Pane by clicking the Notebook Pane arrow to the left of the first Section tab (refer to Figure 1.5). To keep the pane open, click the pushpin icon at the top right corner of the pane.

Section tabs make it possible to keep different sections or topics within the notebook separated. You might create a notebook for this semester's work titled "Fall Semester." Inside that notebook, you could add sections devoted to each class being taken this semester. Within each section, you might have a general notes page, an assignments page, and a research page. By having different sections, the specific content you need is easy to locate. When you create too many section tabs to display, OneNote adds a tab with a down arrow that enables you to access sections easily that do not show from a list. Even when all section tabs display, a **Section group** gives you the option to organize sections into related groupings.

The **Search box** consists of a text box, a magnifying glass search icon, and a Change Search Scope arrow that provides the option to change **search scope** parameters, which determine where OneNote searches to find key terms. Parameter choices are Find on This Page, This Section, This Section Group, This Notebook, and All Notebooks, with the option to set any of these as the default search scope. These search scope parameters enable you to limit the search to a specific area or notebook. The All Notebooks search parameter should only be used if you do not know which notebook contains the content for which you are searching.

The **Page Pane,** located on the right side of the screen, shows **page tabs** for all pages included in the current selected section. The page area is the actual page to which you will add content. In the top right corner of the page area, there is a diagonal double pointed arrow. This is the Full Page View button. In Full Page view, the Ribbon and Section tabs are hidden. To return to Normal view, click the diagonal pointed arrow Normal View button. **Subpage tabs** are indented below the page tabs to which they are attached. Table 1.1 describes OneNote tools and features.

TABLE 1.1	OneNote 2016 Interface
Tools	**Features**
Quick Access Toolbar	By default, the Quick Access Toolbar contains three commands: Back button, Undo button, and Customize Quick Access Toolbar button.
Ribbon	The Ribbon has seven tabs: File, Home, Insert, Draw, History, Review, and View. The tabs provide easy access to commands for formatting and managing content in your pages.
Notebook Pane	By default, this is minimized. In its maximized position, the Notebook Pane lists notebooks, allowing you to switch easily between notebooks.
Section tabs	The section tabs display the sections in your notebook, and provide an easy way to add a new section.
Section group tabs	Section group tabs are used to move sections into related groupings. This keeps related sections together in one group.
Search box	The Search box allows you to search for content within your notebook.
Page Pane	The Page Pane displays tabs for pages located within the selected section.
Page tabs	Page tabs provide access to the pages in a section.
Page area	The Page Area is the current page displayed in the center of your screen. This is where you will add content to your notebook.

Pearson Education, Inc.

Create a Notebook and Add Sections and Pages

STEP 1 ▸▸ Because OneNote enables you to create as many notebooks as you need, you can create separate notebooks for different purposes. You might create a different notebook for home and family, school, and work. Within each notebook, you can create appropriate sections. For your home and family notebook, you might have a section for family contact information such as phone numbers, addresses, birthdays, a chores section, and another section to keep track of appointments. For the school notebook, you might have a section for each class with pages for lecture notes, homework, research, and schedules. For your work notebook, you might have a section for coworkers where you have pages for phone numbers, a section for project notes and target dates, and another for team activities. New notebooks are created in Backstage view (see Figure 1.7). The first time you create a new notebook, OneNote automatically creates a OneNote Notebooks folder where the notebook is saved. Subsequent notebooks will be saved to this folder as the default, unless you specify another location.

> **To create a new notebook, complete the following steps:**
>
> 1. Click File to open Backstage view, and click New.
> 2. Navigate to the location where the notebook should be saved in the New Notebook window, such as your storage device or OneDrive.
> 3. Name the notebook.
> 4. Click Create Notebook.

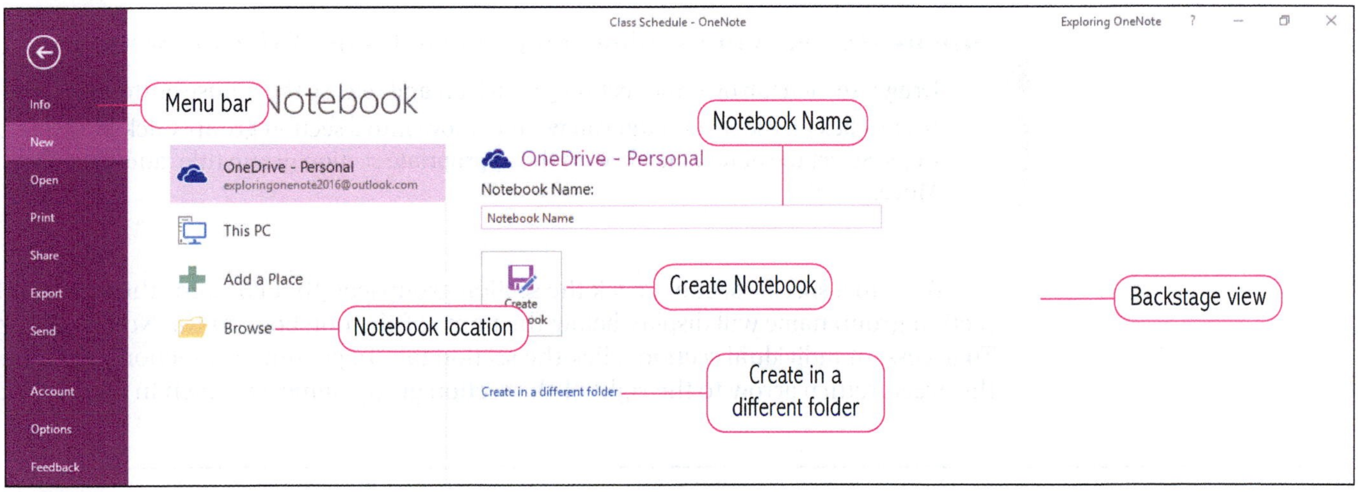

FIGURE 1.7 Backstage View

Before opening your newly created notebook, OneNote displays a message box giving you the option to *share* your notebook. If you want to share, click Invite people, and enter the email address of the person with whom you want to share. If you invite someone to share your notebook, OneNote will save your notebook to your OneDrive to make it possible to share the notebook. If not, click Not now. Your new notebook opens with a default section titled New Section 1. The default section contains one Untitled page. You can add additional sections and pages to accommodate your needs.

> **To add a new section, complete one of the following steps:**
>
> • Right-click on an existing Section tab, and click New Section.
> • Click the small tab with a (+) sign on it.

To add a new page to a section, complete one of the following steps:

- Right-click on an existing page tab, and click New Page.
- Click the Add Page command at the top of the Page Pane.
- Press Ctrl+N.

To make a page into a subpage, right-click on the Page tab, and click Make Subpage.

Group Notebook Sections

STEP 2 Although OneNote 2016 does enable you to create as many notebooks as you desire, juggling multiple notebooks can be difficult. Because OneNote also enables you to have as many sections and pages as you need in each notebook, you could create one notebook, and then group the sections to keep related sections together. A section group can hold an unlimited number of sections.

To group sections, complete the following steps:

1. Right-click a section tab or the white space to the right of the last section tab.
2. Click New Section Group.
3. Type the section group name.
4. Press Enter. The section group will display to the right of the section tabs.

To move sections into a section group, complete one of the following steps:

- Drag a section tab over the section group icon and release the mouse button.
- Right-click on the section tab you want to move into a section group. Click Move or Copy. Select the notebook, click on the appropriate section group title, and then click Move.

To go to a specific section, click the section group icon that contains the section. The section group name will display below the name of the notebook in the Notebook Pane. To access an individual section, click the section tab. To get out of a section group, click the green return arrow to the right of the section group name as shown in Figure 1.8.

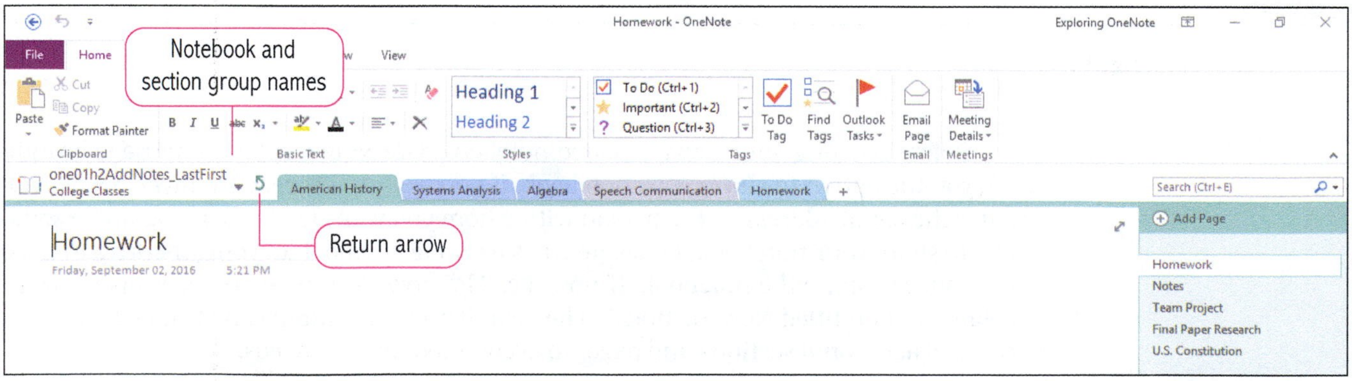

OneNote 2016, Windows 10, Microsoft Corporation

FIGURE 1.8 Section Groups

Rename and Delete Sections and Pages

STEP 3 When a new section is created, the default name is New Section (#) where # is replaced by a number. Each time you create a new section, the number will increment to the next higher number. Each new section has a default page named Untitled Page. The default name of a new section is highlighted to indicate that you can type a new name to replace the default text. If you click off the tab, you will have to use a different method to rename the section. Section and page names should represent the content in them. If you copy and paste a section to a new notebook or copy and paste a page into a different section, you may need to change the name. With multiple ways to complete renaming and deleting sections, you can select the method that works best for the way you work.

To rename a section or page, complete one of the following steps:

- Right-click the Section tab or Page tab, and click Rename. Type the new name, and press Enter.
- Double-click the Section tab, type the new name, and then press Enter.
- Triple-click the page name in the page area, type the new name, and then press Enter.

You may find that you have added too many sections or pages, or have sections and pages that are no longer needed. Removing unwanted sections and pages keeps your notebook cleaner and easier to use. There are three methods that can be used to delete a section or a page.

To delete a section or page, complete one of the following steps:

- Right-click the Section tab or Page tab (see Figure 1.9), and click Delete.
- Select the Page tab, and click Delete on the Home tab in the Basic Text group.
- Select the Page tab, and press Delete.

OneNote 2016, Windows 10, Microsoft Corporation

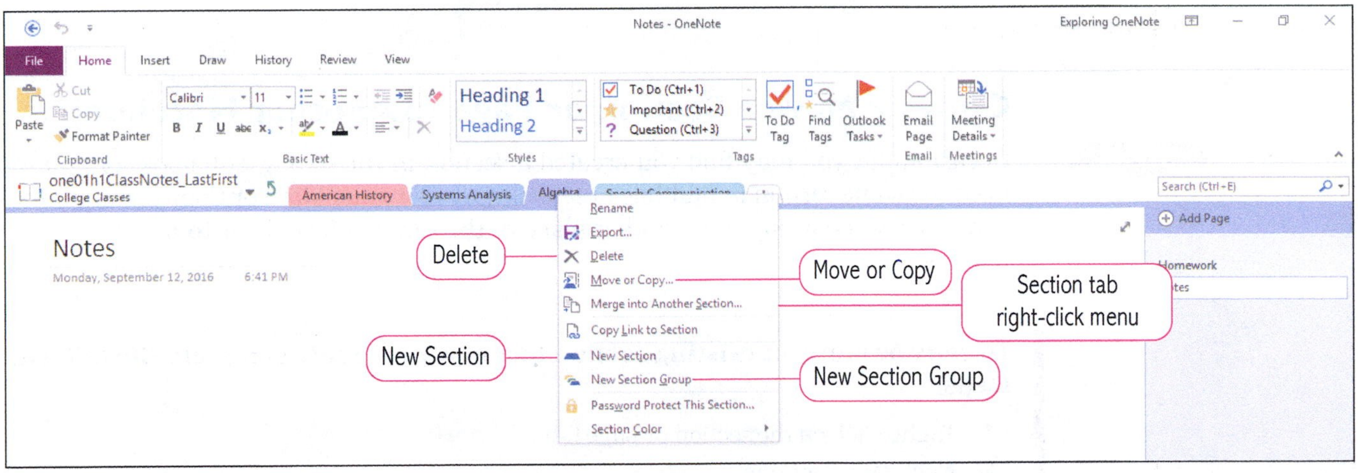

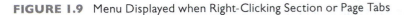

FIGURE 1.9 Menu Displayed when Right-Clicking Section or Page Tabs

If a section or page is accidentally deleted, you can retrieve the section or page until the Recycle Bin has been emptied.

To retrieve a section or page you deleted, complete the following steps:

1. Click the History tab.
2. Click the upper half of the Notebook Recycle Bin in the History group.
3. Select the section or page you need to retrieve.
4. Right-click the tab of the section or page, and use the Move or Copy command to move the section or page back to the original notebook.
5. Click the green return arrow to the right of the Recycle Bin name to exit the Recycle Bin.

If you do not find the section or page you want to retrieve, make sure you are in the notebook from which the section or page was deleted. Each notebook has its own separate Recycle Bin. The name of the Recycle Bin displays below the notebook name (see Figure 1.10).

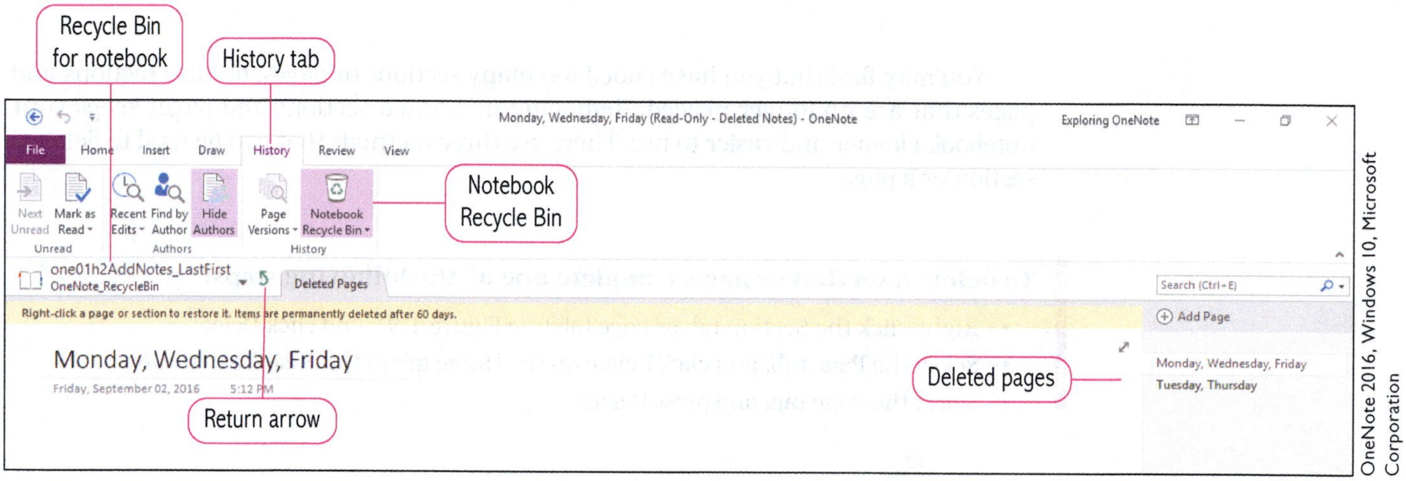

FIGURE 1.10 The Notebook Recycle Bin

Copy or Move a Section or Page to Another Notebook

STEP 4 ❱❱ Occasionally, you may find you created a section in the wrong notebook, or you may need the same section in multiple notebooks. By using the Move or Copy command, you can move or copy pages to another place in the same notebook, or to another existing notebook.

To copy or move an existing section to a new notebook, complete the following steps:

1. Right-click on the section or page tab.
2. Click Move or Copy.
3. Select the notebook to which you want to copy the section.
4. Click Move or click Copy.

If you copy a section to another notebook, the original section remains in the original notebook. If you move the section, the original notebook no longer contains the section (see Figure 1.11).

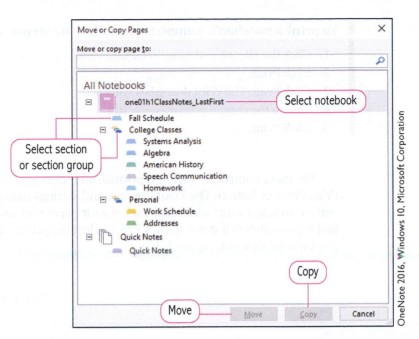

FIGURE 1.11 Move or Copy Pages Dialog Box

OneNote 2016, Windows 10, Microsoft Corporation

Rearrange Sections and Pages, and Merge Sections

STEP 5 ›› New sections are added to the right of existing section tabs. When a new section is added, it might be more logical to have that section as the first tab. To rearrange section tabs, click the section tab and drag the tab to the desired location. As shown in Figure 1.12, an arrow will show where the section will be moved when you release the mouse button. Within sections, page tabs can be rearranged, too. Click and drag the page tab to the new location. There may be times when it makes sense to combine two or more sections. To *merge* a section with another section, right-click the section you want to merge, click Merge into Another Section, select the section you want the section to merge with, and then click Merge.

FIGURE 1.12 Rearranging Sections

OneNote 2016, Windows 10, Microsoft Corporation

Save, Print, and Print Preview a Notebook

STEP 6 ›› If you are familiar with Microsoft Office, you are used to saving your work manually. However, OneNote does not have manual Save functions. OneNote automatically saves your notebook to your chosen saved location. When you are done working with your notebook, simply close OneNote. Your work will be there when you come back to the notebook.

There may be times you need to print your notebook. You may want to have your notes in a more portable format.

To print a notebook, complete the following steps:

1. Click the File tab to display Backstage view.
2. Click Print.
3. Click Print. The Print dialog box will open.
4. Ensure the correct printer is selected.
5. Click Print.

For more control over what is printed, after clicking Print in Backstage view, click the Print Preview button. The Print Preview and Settings dialog box will open, giving you the options to select your print range, select your paper size and orientation, and add a footer and page numbers if desired, click Print, select the printer, and then complete the steps to print a notebook (see Figure 1.13).

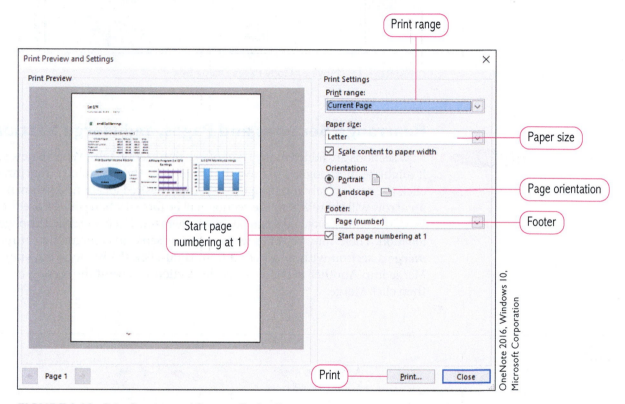

FIGURE 1.13 Print Preview and Settings Dialog Box

Send Notes from OneNote using Outlook

When working with a team, OneNote makes it easy to keep classmates and coworkers updated. Sharing class notes with fellow students or meeting notes with coworkers is easily accomplished by sending notes through email. To do this, you must have Outlook 2013 or Outlook 2016 set up on your computer. By clicking Email Page in the Email group on the Home tab, a new Outlook email will generate with the page attached. Fill in the recipient's email address, a subject, and any message, before sending the email.

When your Outlook account is established, an additional group, Meetings, displays at the right end of the OneNote 2016 Home tab. The Meeting Details command enables you to review the details of appointments and meetings set up in your Outlook account, as shown in Figure 1.14.

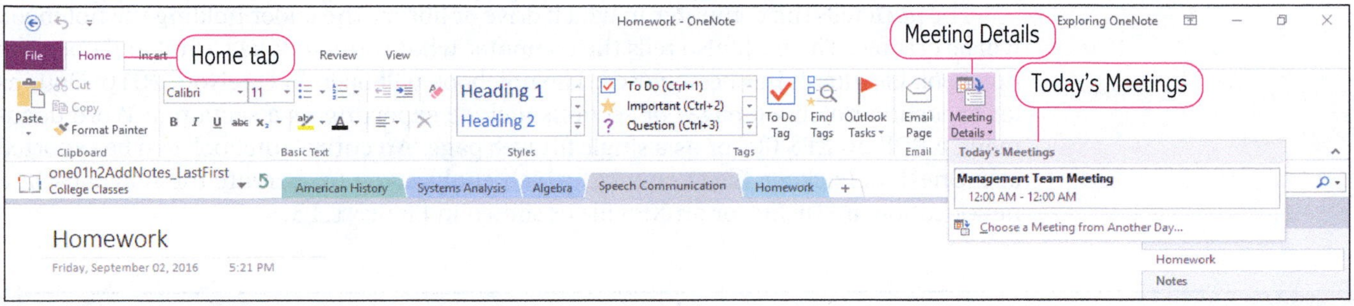

OneNote 2016, Windows 10, Microsoft Corporation

FIGURE 1.14 Outlook Appointment and Meeting Details

If you do not have Outlook 2013 or 2016, you can still send notes by email, but you will have to use the Export command to select a page, section, or notebook to export to your hard drive. Once you have exported the file, you can manually attach the exported file to your email. The Export command is also useful for making a backup of your notebook.

Export a Notebook

While sharing a OneNote notebook with others is a good way to provide business essential information to team members and colleagues, there are times when you will need to save a backup of the notebook to a different storage media than your hard drive. Having a backup of your notebook is essential, just as it is for all other computer files and data. If your tablet or laptop is lost or stolen, you can use the backup to restore your notebook, as long as the backup is stored somewhere other than your hard drive. Using the ***Export*** command in Backstage view, you can save the entire notebook, a page, a group, or a section to a different location. Another reason to use Export would be to create a new notebook based on a previous notebook. This reduces the time to create a new notebook, and gives you a basic structure with which to work.

To export an entire notebook, complete the following steps:

1. Open the notebook to be exported.
2. Click the File tab.
3. Click Export.
4. Select Notebook in the Export Current section.
5. Select OneNote Package (*.onepkg) in the Select Format section.
6. Click Export.
7. Navigate to the correct storage device.
8. Change the file name if desired.
9. Click Save.

To open (unpack) an exported notebook file (*.onepkg), complete the following steps:

1. Use File Explorer to navigate to the location to which the exported file was saved.
2. Double-click the file name.
3. Verify the name of the notebook in the Unpack Notebook dialog box.
4. Verify the path to the notebook location where you want the notebook created.
5. Click Create.

The **path** tells the computer in which drive or library the folder holding the notebook will be created. The path also tells the computer what route to take to find and open the notebook file after it has been closed. The notebook will open in OneNote 2016. Options for exporting notebook pages or sections include exporting as a section, a Word document, a PDF, an XPS file, or as a single file web page. An entire notebook can be exported as a OneNote Package file (*.onepkg) which enables you to recreate the notebook in a new location, a PDF file, or an XPS file as shown in Figure 1.15.

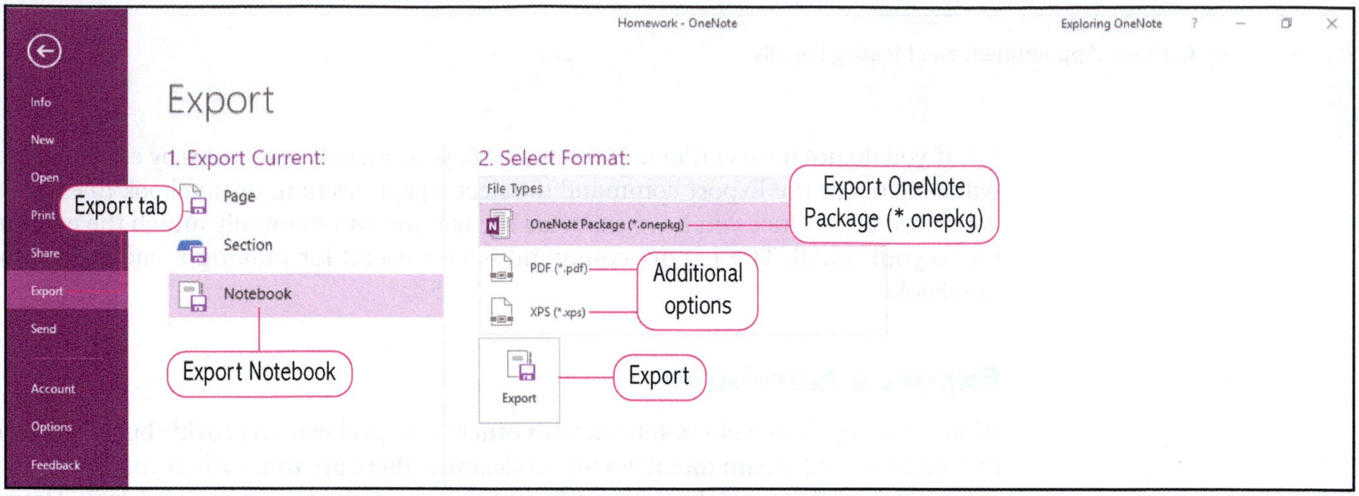

FIGURE 1.15 Export an Entire Notebook

Email a Note into OneNote 2016

Previously, you learned how to email a OneNote page, section, or notebook to someone else. A new feature of OneNote 2016 enables you to email content into your own notebook using your email account. Using this function, you can forward quick notes, photos you take with your phone, important emails, or a task list to your notebook. For instance, you might take a photo of a historical marker at the side of the road, and email the photo to your notebook for inclusion in an American History report. To email notes into a notebook, you must have a Microsoft account, and you will have to set up your email address(es) to work with OneNote 2016.

To enable your email address(es), complete the following steps:

1. Go to https://www.onenote.com/emailsettings and sign into your Microsoft account.
2. Select the email address(es) you want to enable. To add another email address, click Add another address.
3. Choose a default notebook and section for your emails to be saved to.
4. Click Save.

TIP: CONFIRMING YOUR EMAIL ADDRESS
If you have not previously confirmed your email address with Microsoft, you may be required to do so before using your email to send notes to OneNote. To do this, open Outlook and open the email from the Outlook Team with the subject line: Almost there! Confirm your email address for me@onenote.com. Click Confirm Email Address, and follow the instructions on the screen (see Figures 1.16–1.18).

> **TIP: SAVING TO A DIFFERENT SECTION IN THE DEFAULT NOTEBOOK**
>
> To email content to a specific section in the default notebook, type the @ symbol, and then type the section name, with no spaces between the @ symbol and the section name in the subject line.
>
> Example: To: me@OneNote.com
> Subject: @Algebra

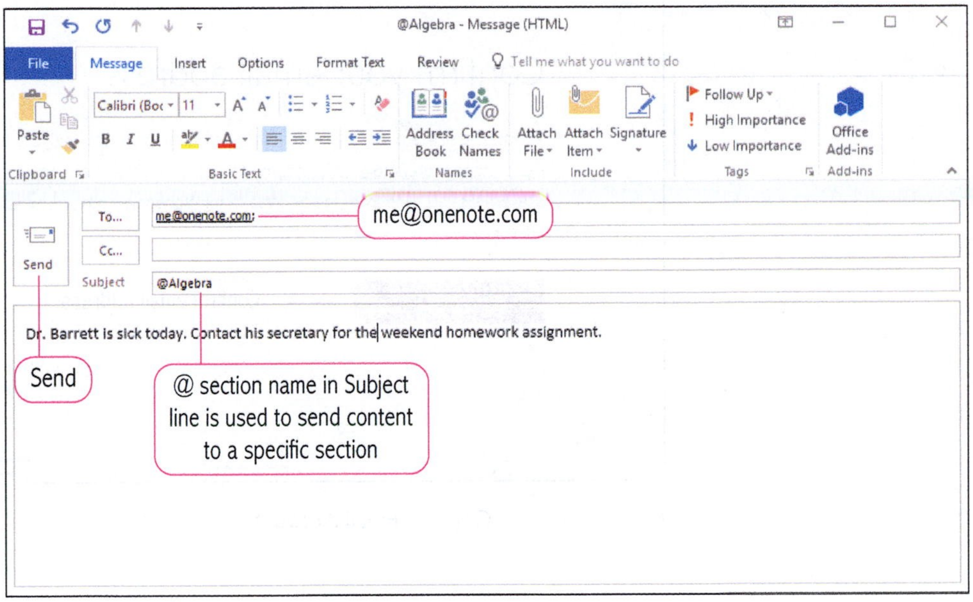

Outlook 2016, Windows 10, Microsoft Corporation

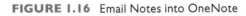

FIGURE 1.16 Email Notes into OneNote

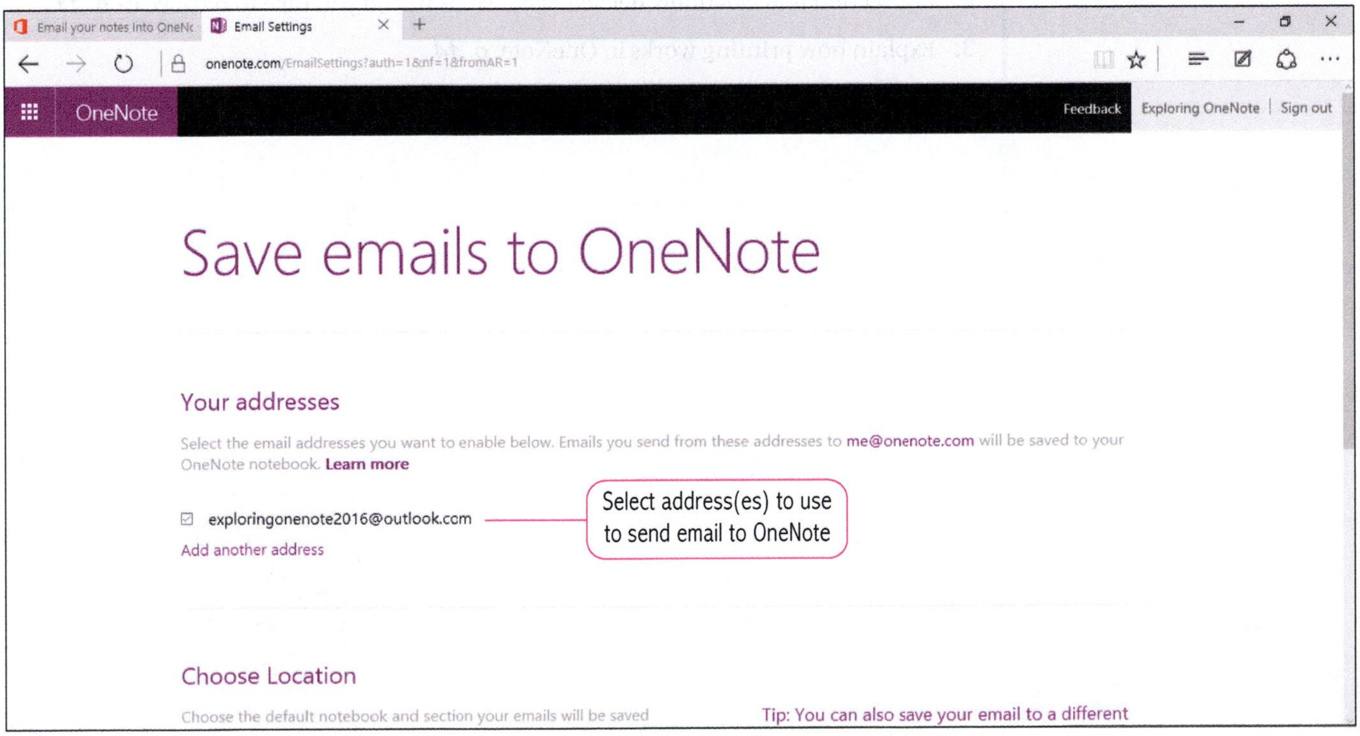

OneNote 2016, Windows 10, Microsoft Corporation

FIGURE 1.17 Save Email to OneNote

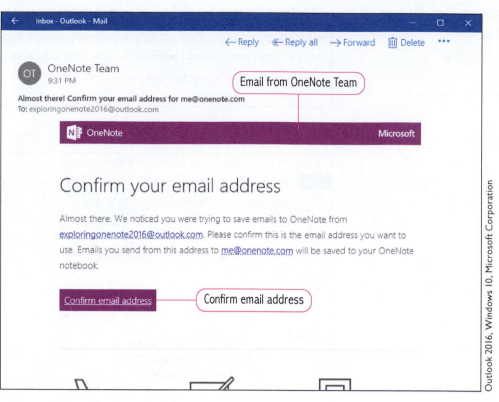

FIGURE 1.18 Confirm Email Account

Quick Concepts

1. What sections and pages would you create in a notebook for personal information? *p. 9*

2. If a section is accidentally deleted, what steps would you take to retrieve it? *p. 11*

3. Explain how printing works in OneNote. *p. 14*

4. List two reasons you might need to export a notebook to a USB drive. *p. 15*

Hands-On Exercises

Skills covered: Create a Notebook • Add Sections
• Add Pages • Add Subpages Group Notebook Sections
• Rename Sections • Rename Pages • Delete Sections
• Delete Pages • Undelete Sections • Undelete Pages
• Copy a Section to Another Notebook • Rearrange
Sections • Rearrange Pages • Add a Footer • Print a
Section • Send a Section • Export a Notebook

1 Introduction to OneNote 2016

After providing a short introduction to OneNote, Dr. Singh recommended that Bonnie create a notebook to keep track of her school courses. You have offered to help Bonnie create her notebook and set it up to be useful.

STEP 1 ➤➤ **CREATE A NOTEBOOK AND ADD SECTIONS AND PAGES**

After creating a notebook for course work, you will add course sections and pages to the notebook. Please note that tab colors will differ from the tabs in the figures. When you save files, use your last and first names. For example, as the OneNote author, I would name my notebook "one01h1ClassNotes_PogueLinda." Refer to Figure 1.19 as you complete Step 1.

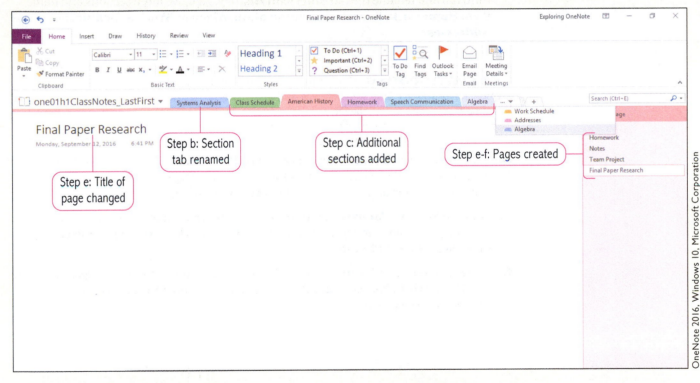

FIGURE 1.19 School Courses Notebook

> **TROUBLESHOOTING:** If you make any major mistakes in this exercise, close OneNote. In File Explorer, navigate to where you saved your notebook. Open the OneNote Notebooks folder that OneNote automatically created for you. Locate and select the notebook folder for the notebook you are working with, and press Delete on the keyboard. Reopen OneNote, and start this exercise over.

a. Open **OneNote 2016.** Click **File**, and click **New.** Select **Browse**, click the **Browse** button, and then navigate to the location where you want to save your notebook. Type **one01h1ClassNotes_LastFirst** in the Notebook Name box, where LastFirst is replaced by your Last and First name. Click **Create**. If a message displays asking you if you want to share the notebook, select **Not now**.

> **TROUBLESHOOTING:** If you do not use Browse or the Create in a different folder link, you will be presented with a Create Notebook button. Click Browse and navigate to the location where you want to save your notebook, and follow the steps above.

b. Right-click the **New Section 1 tab** in OneNote, click **Rename**, type **Systems Analysis**, and then press **Enter**.

> **TROUBLESHOOTING:** Are your section tabs a different color than those in the figures? If a color scheme is not selected when the notebook is created, OneNote determines the color scheme. Your color scheme may vary from that shown in the textbook figures. If you want to change the color of your section tabs, right-click the section tab you want to change, click Section Color, and then select the color you want.

c. Click the **Create a New Section tab**. Rename the new tab **Class Schedule**. Create a third tab and rename the tab **American History**. Add five more sections and name them **Homework**, **Speech Communication**, **Algebra**, **Work Schedule**, and **Addresses**.

> **TROUBLESHOOTING:** Depending on the number of tabs you have in a notebook, and the resolution of your monitor, some of your section tabs may not display. You will find them in the list that displays when you click the tab with the arrow.

d. Click the **Class Schedule Section tab**. Type **Monday, Wednesday, Friday** in the title area on the Untitled page. Click **Add Page**, above the Page tab. Ensure the insertion point is in the title area and name it **Tuesday, Thursday**.

e. Click the **Systems Analysis Section tab**. Type **Team Project** in the title area on the Untitled page. Add four pages and title them **Homework**, **Final Paper Research**, **Class Schedule**, and **Notes**.

f. Add **Homework** and **Notes** pages to the Speech Communication and Algebra sections. Add **Homework**, **Notes**, **Team Project**, and **Final Paper Research** pages to the American History section.

STEP 2 » GROUP NOTEBOOK SECTIONS

Bonnie has decided to use only one notebook, rather than keep up with one for school and one for personal content. After discussing it with her, you have offered to create section groups to make it easier to keep the different types of information separated. Refer to Figure 1.20 as you complete Step 2.

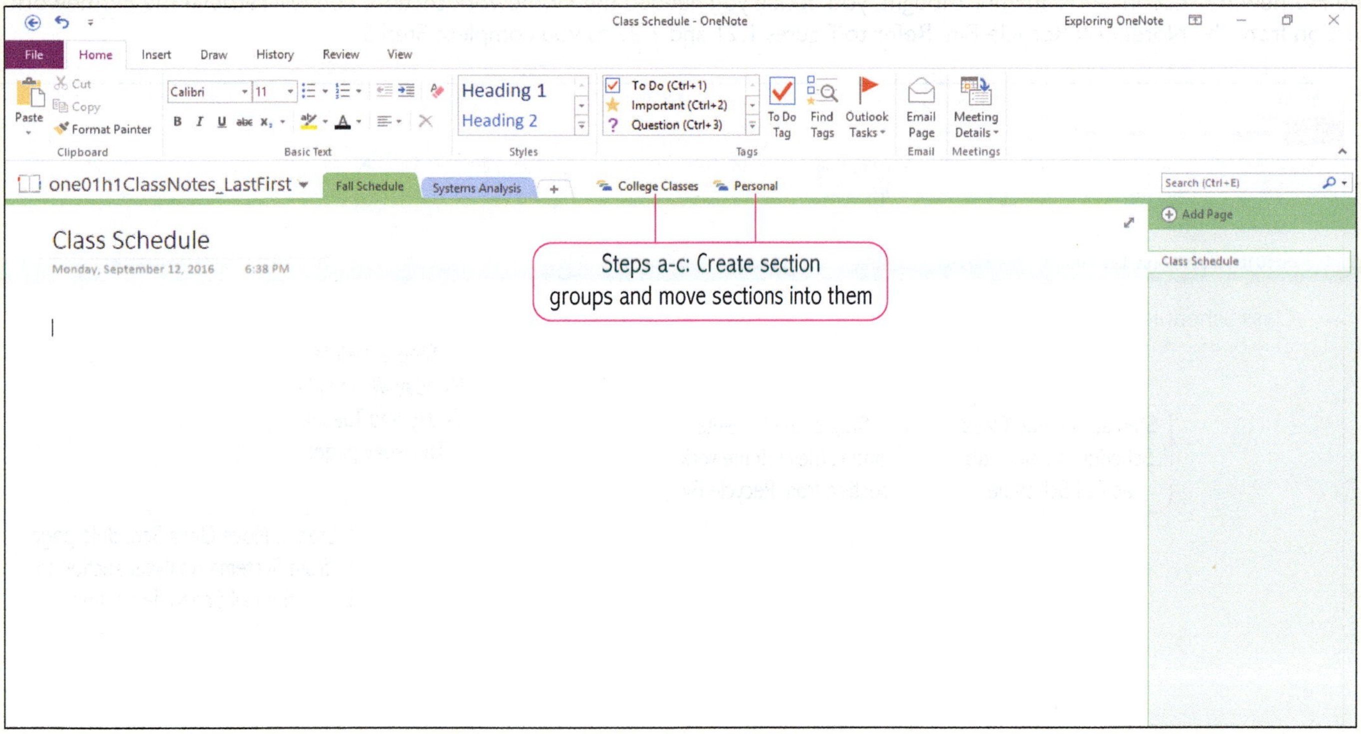

OneNote 2016, Windows 10, Microsoft Corporation

FIGURE 1.20 College Classes and Personal Section Groups

a. Right-click the white space to the right of the Create a New Section tab, and click **New Section Group**. Type **College Classes** for the section group name, and press **Enter**.

b. Add another section group named **Personal**. Drag the **American History, Speech Communication**, and **Algebra** section tabs, one at a time, onto the College Classes group section icon.

c. Drag the **Work Schedule** and **Addresses** section tabs onto the Personal section group icon. Click the **Return arrow** to return to the parent notebook.

TROUBLESHOOTING: If the section group icon you need in the steps above is in the list, drag the section tab to the down arrow tab. When the list displays, drop the tab on top of the group section icon. If the College Classes section group opens when you drag and drop a section onto the section group icon, click the green return arrow to the left of the section tabs to return to the main notebook.

After reviewing the notebook section groups, sections, and pages, you realize you do not need separate pages for the Monday, Wednesday, Friday classes and Tuesday, Thursday classes. You decide to delete the Monday, Wednesday, Friday classes page and the Tuesday, Thursday classes page, and move the Class Schedule page to the Class Schedule section and rename it as Fall Schedule section. After thinking a bit, you decide that each class section should have a separate homework page, so you will delete the Homework section. After further thought, you decide you needed the Homework section. You will retrieve the Homework section from the Notebook Recycle Bin. Refer to Figures 1.21 and 1.22 as you complete Step 3.

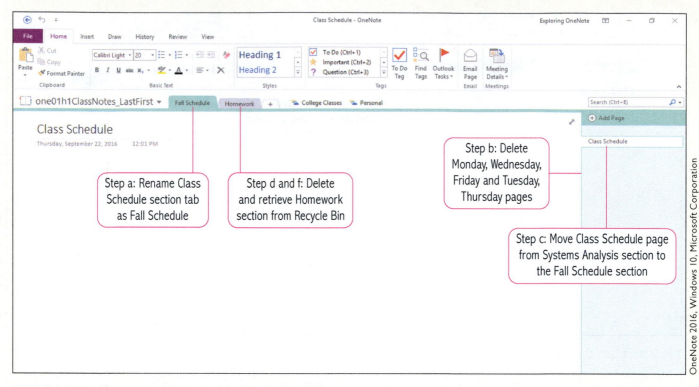

FIGURE 1.21 Notebook with Sections and Section Groups

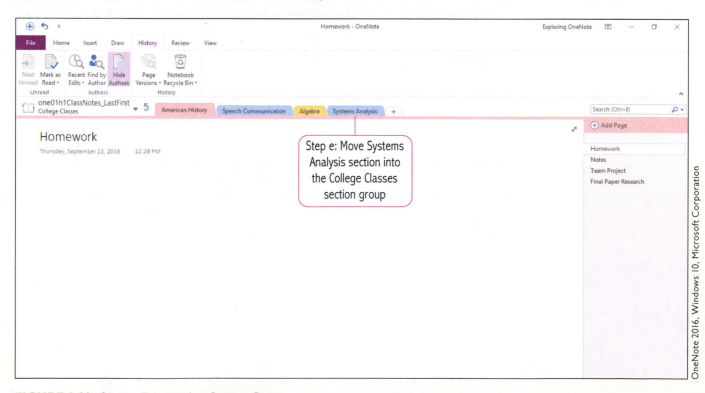

FIGURE 1.22 Section Tabs inside a Section Group

a. Right-click the **Class Schedule Section tab**. Click **Rename**, type **Fall Schedule**, and then press **Enter**.

b. Right-click the **Monday, Wednesday, Friday page tab**, and click **Delete**. Right-click the **Tuesday, Thursday page tab**, and click **Delete**.

> **TROUBLESHOOTING:** If a message displays asking if you want to continue, click Yes.

c. Click the **Systems Analysis Section tab**. Right-click the **Class Schedule Page tab**. Click **Move or Copy**. Make sure your **one01h1ClassNotes_LastFirst** notebook is selected in the Move or Copy Pages dialog box. Click the **expand (+) button** to the left of the notebook name, if the section tab names do not display. Select the **Fall Schedule Section tab**, and click **Move**.

d. Right-click the **Homework Section tab**. Click **Delete**. Click **Yes** if a message displays asking if you are sure.

e. Ensure the main notebook is displayed. Drag the **Systems Analysis Section tab** on top of the College Classes section group icon.

f. Click the **History tab**. Click **Notebook Recycle Bin** in the History group. Right-click the **Homework section tab**, and click **Move or Copy**. Select the **one01h1ClassNotes_LastFirst** notebook. Click **Move**. Rename the Untitled page as **Weekly Homework**.

STEP 4 ›› COPY A SECTION TO ANOTHER NOTEBOOK

Bonnie showed her new notebook to Jon Michaels. Jon asked her to set up a OneNote notebook for him using the exact same sections and pages. Bonnie has asked you to help her create Jon's notebook. Refer to Figure 1.23 as you complete Step 4.

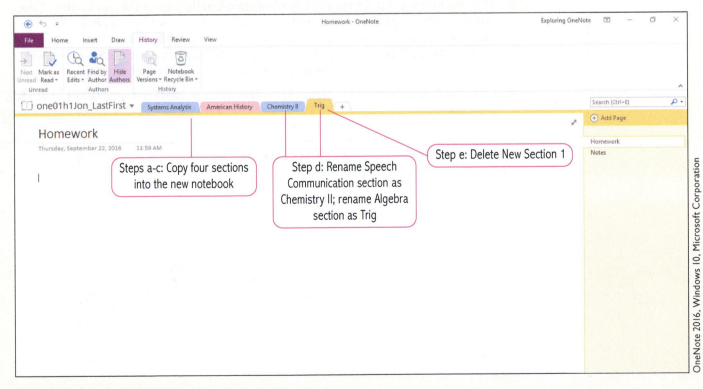

FIGURE 1.23 Sections Copied from a Different Notebook

a. Click the **File tab**, and click **New**. Click **This PC**. Click **Create in a different folder**, navigate to your storage device, click **New folder**, name the folder **Exploring OneNote**, click **Open**, type **one01h1Jon_LastFirst** in the Notebook Name text box, and then click **Create**. Click **Not now** if a message displays asking if you want to share the notebook.

b. Click the **arrow** to the left of the first Section tab to open the Navigation pane to display all open notebooks. Click **one01h1ClassNotes_LastFirst** to reopen the original notebook.

c. Select the **College Classes group** in your one01h1ClassNotes_LastFirst notebook. Right-click the **Systems Analysis Section tab**. Click **Move or Copy**. Select **one01h1Jon_LastFirst**, and click **Copy**. Use the same method to copy the remaining section tabs to one01h1Jon_LastFirst.

> **TROUBLESHOOTING:** If you clicked Move instead of Copy, use the same method to copy the section back to the one01h1ClassNotes_LastFirst notebook.

d. Click **one01h1Jon_LastFirst** in the Navigation pane. Whereas Jon shares most of your classes, instead of Speech Communication, he is taking Chemistry II. Rename the Speech Communication section as **Chemistry II**. Jon is taking Trigonometry instead of Algebra, so rename the Algebra Section tab **Trig**.

e. Right-click **New Section 1** in one01h1Jon_LastFirst, and click **Delete**. Click **Yes** if a message displays asking if you are sure.

> **TIP: PIN THE NOTEBOOK PANE**
> To keep the Notebook Pane open, click the Pin Notebook Pane to Side icon in the top right corner of the pane. To close a pinned Notebook Pane, click the pin icon again.

f. Click the **File tab**. Click **Export**. Select **Notebook** in the Export Current section. Select **OneNote Package (*.onepkg)** in the Select Format section. Click **Export**. Verify the file name in the Save As dialog box File Name box is one01h1Jon_LastFirst, and the Save as File Type selected is OneNote Single File Package, and click **Save.** You will submit this file to your instructor at the end of the last Hands-On Exercise.

g. Open the **Navigation Pane**. Right-click **one01h1Jon_LastFirst**, and click **Close This Notebook**.

> **TROUBLESHOOTING:** Your section tabs may have different colors than those shown in Figure 1.23 and may be in a different order.

Bonnie has decided to rearrange the sections in order of her classes, Monday, Wednesday, Friday classes first, and then in order of scheduled time, and then Tuesday, Thursday classes. Refer to Figure 1.24 as you complete Step 5.

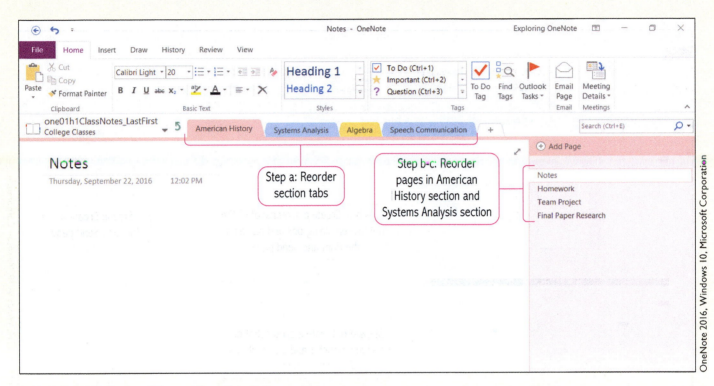

FIGURE 1.24 Section Tabs and Page Tabs Rearranged

a. Click the **fourth section tab** in the College Courses section group, hold the left mouse button and drag the tab to the left until a small arrow displays above and to the left of the first section tab. Release the left mouse button. Use the same technique to rearrange the sections in the order listed below:

American History

Systems Analysis

Algebra

Speech Communication

b. Click the **Systems Analysis section tab**, and select the **Notes page tab**. Hold down the left mouse button and drag the tab to the top of the list. The pages should be in Notes, Homework, Team Project, and Final Paper Research order.

c. Click the **American History section tab**, and select the **Notes** page tab. Change the order of the pages to Notes, Homework, Team Project, and Final Paper Research.

d. Change the order of the pages in the Algebra and Speech Communications sections to Notes, and Homework.

Bonnie has decided to print the Systems Analysis section for easy reference when she does not have access to her computer. She has decided that she needs page numbers to appear in the footer for each page, in case the pages are dropped and are no longer in order. Refer to Figure 1.25 as you complete Step 6.

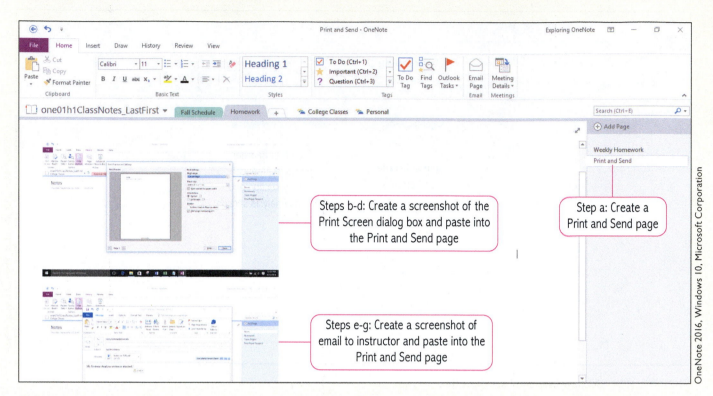

FIGURE 1.25 Screenshots

a. Click the **Homework section tab**. Add a new page titled **Print and Send**.

b. Click the **College Classes section group icon**, click the **Systems Analysis section tab**, and then click the **File tab**. Click **Print**, and click **Print Preview**. Select **Current Page** in the Print range. Make sure Paper size is set to **Letter**, and the **Scale content to paper width** option is selected.

c. Ensure that Portrait orientation is selected. Make sure the Footer selection is Systems Analysis Page (number), and Start page numbering at 1 is selected.

d. Use the arrow buttons at the bottom of the Print Preview pane to scroll through all pages in the section. Return to Page 1. Do not click Print. Use **Windows+PrtScn** to create a screenshot. Click **Close**. Navigate to the **Print and Send page** in the Homework section, and press **Ctrl+V** to paste the screenshot below the page title.

e. Navigate back to the **Systems Analysis section tab**. Click the **File tab**. Click **Send**. Click **Send as PDF**.

f. Type your instructor's email address in the **To box** in the email address form. Change the Subject line to **LastFirst Notes**.

g. Type **My Systems Analysis section is attached.** in the message box. Use **Windows+PrtScn** to create a screenshot. Navigate to the **Print and Send page** in the Homework section, and press **Ctrl+V** to paste the screenshot below the Print Preview screenshot. You will not send the email at this time. Close the email window without saving or sending.

h. Keep OneNote open if you plan to continue with the next Hands-On Exercise. If not, exit OneNote.

OneNote 2016 Content

Research has shown that different learners learn differently. There are auditory learners, people who learn better hearing information, visual learners who learn better by seeing information, and kinesthetic learners, who have to actually use the information or perform a task to learn well. OneNote works equally well for all learning types. Auditory learners can use the recorder to record notes verbally and listen to them later. The actions of reading aloud and then hearing the recording both help the auditory learner. By using formatting to change colors, highlight, and change font sizes and fonts, visual learners can better learn the information. Typing notes or, with a tablet, handwriting notes helps kinesthetic learners remember lesson material. Regardless of which learning style you possess, OneNote enables you learn in the best way for your style, because you can add color to text (visual), record yourself reading your notes aloud to listen to later (auditory), or use the pen and drawing tools to create small sketches, mind maps, and illustrations (kinesthetic). OneNote 2016 will not allow you to insert files that are larger than 100 MB.

In this section, you will learn how to add notes, screen clips, web information, photos, and files to a OneNote 2016 notebook.

Adding Content to OneNote 2016

One of the best features of OneNote is that you can add so many different types of content. OneNote enables you to add notes by typing, or writing with a finger or stylus if you are using a tablet or touch screen, anywhere in the Page area. To add notes, simply click or tap on the page below the page title and date, then start typing or writing. A ***container*** is added to hold the text you add. Sometimes, however, you need to add more than just typed or written notes (see Figure 1.26).

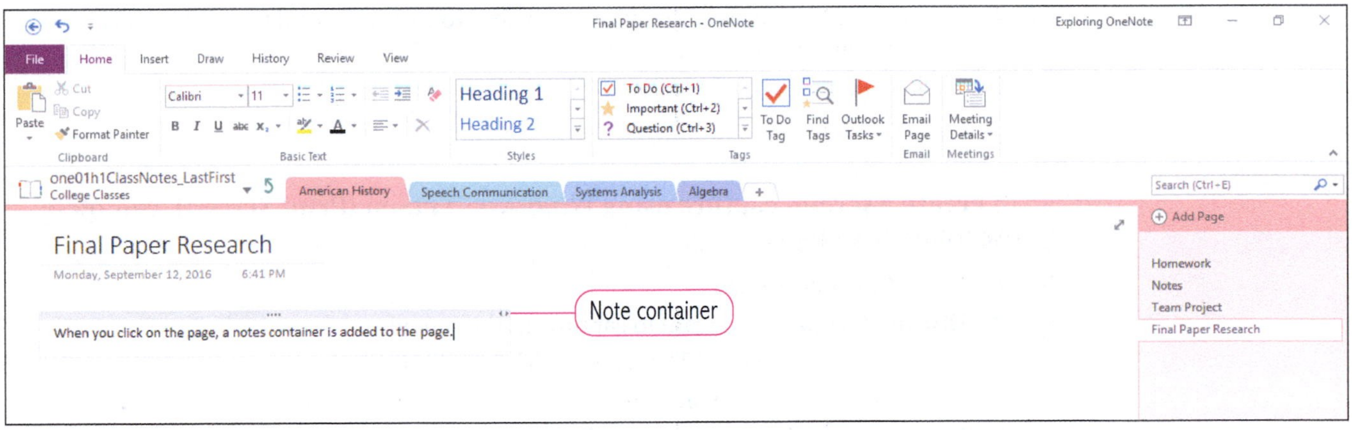

OneNote 2016, Windows 10, Microsoft Corporation

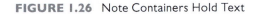

FIGURE 1.26 Note Containers Hold Text

Create Screen Clips

STEP 1 Occasionally, you may need to have an image of content on your screen. A screen clip or ***screenshot*** is a snapshot of your screen that creates an image that can be saved or pasted into Microsoft applications. There are three basic ways to capture screen clips or screenshots for OneNote:

- The keyboard shortcut to the Screen Clipping command, Windows+Shift+S.
- Windows+PrtScn for the Windows 10 Start screen.
- Screen Clipping in the Images group on the Insert tab.

Without purchasing specialized image capture software, there are three ways to get a screen clip into OneNote. The first is Windows+Shift+S. On your keyboard, to the left and right of your spacebar, there is a Windows or Start key. Some keyboards will only have the Windows or Start key on the left side of the spacebar.

The second method is to use Windows+PrtScn. When you use this method, the monitor will briefly flash while Windows 10 takes a screenshot. The screenshot of the Start screen is stored in active memory and is also saved to the Pictures Library in a folder named *Screenshots*. The file will be saved with a default File name of Screenshot (#) where # is replaced by a number. Each time you take a screenshot, the number will increment to the next higher number. You can navigate to the Screenshots folder in the Pictures Library, rename the image file, and move it to the appropriate location. The third method uses the Screen Clipping command available on OneNote's Insert tab.

Whichever method you use, the image is in active memory until another screenshot is captured. This means it can also be pasted into a Word document, PowerPoint presentation, or Excel worksheet. These methods also enable you to use OneNote to take an image of a website and paste it to OneNote. Alternative methods are to use the Snipping Tool in the Windows Accessories folder in the Apps menu, or select and copy information or images on the screen, and paste them into OneNote.

After inserting a screenshot into the selected section or page in OneNote, you can right-click on the image and save it as a .png image file. Navigate to the location to which you want to save the image, type the file name of the image, and then click Save.

To create a screen clip using Windows+Shift+S, complete the following steps:

1. Verify OneNote is open.
2. Display the image you want to capture on the screen, and press Windows+Shift+S.
3. Select a region on the screen to clip.
4. Select the notebook, section, and page where you want to send the clipping using the Select Location in OneNote dialog box.
5. Click Send to Selected Location.

To create a screen capture using Windows+PrtScn (Print Screen), complete the following steps:

1. Verify OneNote is open.
2. Display the image you want to capture on the screen.
3. Press Windows+PrtScn. The screen will briefly dim.
4. Navigate to the section and page where you want to insert the screenshot.
5. Right-click on the page, and click Paste in the shortcut menu.

To use the OneNote Screen Clipping command, complete the following steps:

1. Verify the screen you want to capture is open on your computer.
2. Navigate to the OneNote page where you want to insert the image.
3. Click Screen Clipping in the Images group on the Insert tab.
4. Select the area of the screen to be clipped.

OneNote inserts the clip into the page, with a date and time notation below it. If you need to have a URL, filename, or other reference material for the clip, type or write the appropriate information below the screenshot.

Use the New Quick Note Tool

STEP 2 » The New quick note tool enables you to make a new note in OneNote that can be filed into the appropriate page at a later time. The icon for the New quick note tool is located in the Show hidden icons tray in the system tray at the right end of the taskbar as shown in Figure 1.27.

To create a new note in your notebook using the New quick note tool, complete the following steps:

1. Click the Show hidden icons arrow.
2. Click the New quick note icon. A OneNote notes screen will open.
3. Type new information or paste copied content into the blank note screen. The page will be automatically saved in the Quick Notes section of your notebook.
4. Close the Quick Notes window.

To move the quick notes page to a specific place in the notebook, use the instructions located in *Copy or Move a Section or Page to Another Notebook*.

Windows 10, Microsoft Corporation

FIGURE 1.27 New Quick Note Icon

Insert a Link

Sometimes the information you locate on the Web is too lengthy to insert into your notes. In this instance, you can link to the webpage, rather than inserting a full document or image. You can also link to a section or page within the same or a different notebook. For instance, you might link to another page that has relevant content. An example is linking to a family address page from within a birthday page to make it easier to find addresses to mail greeting cards.

To insert a webpage link into the document, complete the following steps:

1. Navigate to the Web site using your browser.
2. Copy the URL in the browser address bar.
3. Display OneNote, and click Link in the Links group on the Insert tab.
4. Type the text that will become the text of the link.
5. Paste the URL in the Address text box.
6. Click OK.

> **To link to a location within OneNote, complete the following steps:**
>
> 1. Click Link in the Links group on the Insert tab.
> 2. Click the expand button (+) to the left of the appropriate notebook.
> 3. Click the expand button (+) to the left of the appropriate section.
> 4. Select the page to which you want to link.
> 5. Click OK.

Paste or Insert a Photo

STEP 3 ›› You may have heard the English idiom "A picture is worth a thousand words." Some of your professors will want images in the reports you write. For instance, a science professor may want a photo of a cell, an economics professor might want a chart of economic growth, a history professor may want a historical photograph, or a computer instructor may want a program development image. Adding the photo or image to your notebook class notes makes it easy to find when it is time to insert it into a report. Be sure to add source information if OneNote does not automatically add it.

Source information is required in any student paper or report to prevent plagiarism. *Plagiarism* is the use of another's ideas or creative work without crediting the owner of the idea or work. Copyright laws provide the framework for decisions as to whether you can legally use another person's content. The *fair use* provision allows limited copying for commenting, criticizing, or supporting a statement. There is no hard and fast rule as to how much can be used in fair use, but generally the less you use the better it is. In your school reports, properly providing source information is usually enough. Copyright laws cover text, illustrations, artwork, and photographs. Not only can you be held legally liable if you plagiarize, you may face the sanctions noted in your school student conduct policies or student handbook.

To paste a photo, it must first be stored in the computer's *clipboard*, a section of memory set aside to hold temporary items. Copying a photo or illustration, or taking a screenshot puts the screen image into the clipboard.

> **To paste a screenshot or copied image into OneNote, complete the following steps:**
>
> 1. Click on the notebook page where you want the image to be placed.
> 2. Click Paste in the Clipboard group on the Home tab.

An alternate method of pasting items from the clipboard is to click on the notebook page where you want the image to be placed, then press Ctrl+V. When images or text are copied from the Internet and pasted into OneNote using the steps above, OneNote inserts the URL source from which the content came.

> **To insert saved pictures, complete the following steps:**
>
> 1. Click Pictures in the Images group on the Insert tab.
> 2. Navigate to the location where the file is saved, select the file, and then click Insert. The image is inserted into the page.

> **To insert an online photo or picture, complete the following steps:**
>
> 1. Click Online Pictures in the Images group on the Insert tab.
> 2. Select Bing Image Search, or your OneDrive, if you are logged in to OneDrive.
> 3. Type keywords into the appropriate text box. Press Enter. Select one or more images, and click Insert.

To select more than one image, hold down the Ctrl key while selecting. The images are inserted into a OneNote page. The source is not inserted along with the image when using the Online Pictures command. Photos can also be attached to your notebook page using the instructions in the Attach a File section.

> **TIP: USING ONENOTE ON YOUR SMARTPHONE**
> If you have the OneNote Mobile app installed on your Smartphone or tablet, you can use the camera to take a photo and add it to your notes. To learn more about using OneNote Mobile on your phone, visit https://support.microsoft.com/en-us/, and search for *OneNote on my phone*.

Convert Text from an Image

STEP 4 ›› One of the exciting features of OneNote is the ability to convert text from images. What this means is that instead of taking time to take notes from a whiteboard or chalkboard during a class or business lecture, you can take a photo of the notes on the board with a digital camera, or you could use the built-in camera in your mobile device to take a still image, and then use OneNote's built-in *optical character recognition (OCR)* capability to convert the image to text notes that can be annotated or tagged as needed (see Figure 1.28). Optical character recognition software is a computer program that converts text in scanned documents and photographs into text. OCR software is not foolproof, and most of the time the converted text will need to have corrections made (see Figures 1.28–1.30).

To convert an image containing text into text, complete the following steps:

1. Insert the scanned image or photo into your notes page area.
2. Right-click on the image, and select Copy Text from Picture.
3. Paste the text from the image into a new container on the same or a new notes page.
4. Make necessary spelling, spacing, and formatting changes.

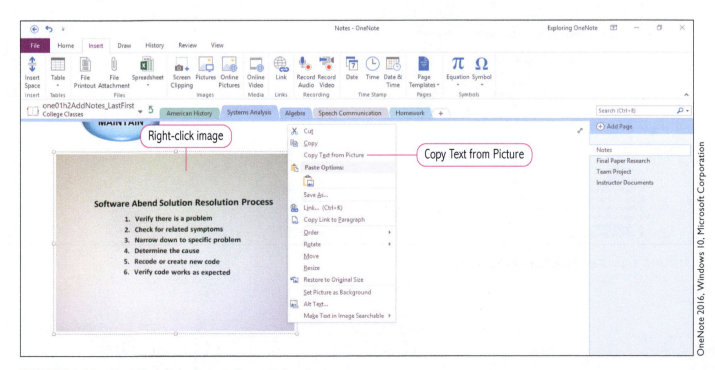

FIGURE 1.28 Copy Text from Picture Command

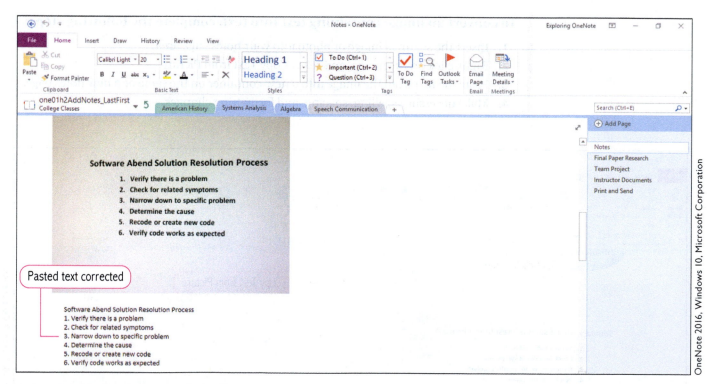

FIGURE 1.29 Mistakes in Text Copied from Picture

FIGURE 1.30 Text from Picture Corrected

The converted text pasted into the page can be edited and formatted in the same way as text you typed into the page. For best results, crop the image to include only the part of the image you desire to convert to text. If you do not have a graphics program, you can do this in Paint, an accessory application that comes with Windows, or in Word. After cropping the image in Word, right-click the image, and click Save as Picture. Save as you would any file.

Record or Embed Media Files to a Page

OneNote provides the option to record or embed media files, such as audio and video. Using OneNote to record audio of lecture notes, either you reading the text and recording it or recording your professor's lecture, auditory learners can enhance their learning, because the recording can be listened to multiple times to help them retain the information. Visual learners can similarly enrich their studies by watching video of the professor's lectures. With your digital device with a camera or webcam, you can record both audio and video from within OneNote. One of the best features of using OneNote 2016 to record audio or video lectures or meeting notes is the ability to type or write notes (on a touch screen or tablet) during the recording. The notes will be linked to the audio or video created with OneNote.

The two ways to add an audio clip to a OneNote page are recording the audio using the Record Audio button in the Recording group on the Insert tab (see Figure 1.31), or attach an existing audio file to the page using the File Attachment command in the Files group on the Insert tab.

The Record Video command is located in the Recording group on the Insert tab. Attaching a video is accomplished the same way as attaching an audio file. In OneNote 2016, you can also embed an existing Office Mix, Dailymotion, Sway, Vine, Vimeo, or YouTube video into a page. This enables you to search your notes to find specific information in the recording. To play the recording, click the media icon, and then click Play.

Keep in mind that, while the record audio and video functions make it easier to capture recordings of classes and meetings, you should always seek your professor's or supervisor's permission ahead of time. Some people are nervous when audio or video recordings are created, given all the questionable postings to social media.

To record audio or video in OneNote, complete the following steps:

1. Click on the page in OneNote where you want to insert the recording.
2. Click the Insert tab, and click Record Audio or Record Video in the Recording group. OneNote adds a media icon to the page and the recording begins.
3. Press Pause or Stop in the Playback group on the Audio & Video Playback contextual tab to end the recording.

To embed an online video file into a page, complete the following steps:

1. Locate the online video you want to embed into OneNote.
2. Copy the video URL or link from the video source.
3. Navigate to the OneNote page where you want to add the video.
4. Click the Insert tab.
5. Click Online Video in the Media group.
6. Paste the link into the Video address field.
7. Click OK.

Another method to add video to a notebook is to copy the URL of an online video, paste the URL into a OneNote page, and press Enter. The video will display after a moment.

OneNote 2016, Windows 10, Microsoft Corporation

FIGURE 1.31 The Insert Tab

Attach a File or Insert a File Printout

There is a difference between attached and inserted content. Inserted content displays in full on the screen similar to a printout of the file. Attached content shows a file icon and the file name. Attaching files of any type is done using commands in the Files group on the Insert tab (refer to Figure 1.31). When a file is attached to the page, it travels with the notebook if you move the notebook to a different computer. To attach a file, click File Attachment in the Files group on the Insert tab. Navigate to where the file is saved on your hard drive, select the file, and then click Insert. In the Insert File dialog box, select whether to attach the file or insert a printout.

To see the content of an attached file, you have to open the file. To open an attached file, either right-click on the file, and click Open, or double-click the file. Because OneNote does not maintain a link to an attached file, if the source file is updated the attached file will not change.

When a file printout is inserted, the entire contents of the file are inserted into OneNote. OneNote treats the inserted file as an image. It can be resized to better fit the page or to make it easier to read by clicking and dragging one of the sizing handles at the corners, top, bottom, or sides.

Create a Table

STEP 5 Tables make it possible to display information in an orderly and logical manner that is easily understood. A table can be as simple as a class schedule or as complicated as a record of grades for school, or a more complex record of department sales in a retail business. In a notebook designed for organizing school work, a table with assignments and due dates would be helpful. Once the table is created, you can move from one cell in the table to the next using the Tab key.

There are three common ways to create a table in OneNote:

- Type the contents of the first cell, then press Tab. OneNote automatically puts the text you typed into a cell and adds another cell to the right. When you have all the cells you need for a row, press Enter to start a new row.

- Use the Table button in the Tables group on the Insert tab to insert a table into a OneNote page. On the Insert tab, in the Tables group, click Table. Drag to select the number of columns and rows you need, and add text.

- Click the Spreadsheet arrow in the Files group on the Insert tab, and select New Excel Spreadsheet. An embedded Excel worksheet displays on the page. Click Edit to open Excel. Type the values and text you need. When you are done, click Close ☒. Click Save. The content you typed into Excel displays in the embedded worksheet. To continue working with the spreadsheet, click Edit again. To finish, click outside the dotted line that indicates the spreadsheet is selected.

Convert a Table to Excel

After you create a table in OneNote, you might decide to insert complicated functions into cells or add conditional formatting. Converting the table to an Excel spreadsheet provides the ability to use all of Excel's features on the table (see Figure 1.32).

To convert a table in OneNote 2016 to an Excel spreadsheet, complete the following steps:

1. Open the page containing the table you want to convert to an Excel spreadsheet.
2. Click inside any cell in the table to display the Layout tab.
3. Click Convert to Excel Spreadsheet in the Convert group. OneNote inserts an Excel file icon on the page and converts the table to an embedded and editable Excel spreadsheet.

Changes made to the spreadsheet file will be automatically updated to the Excel spreadsheet embedded in the OneNote page.

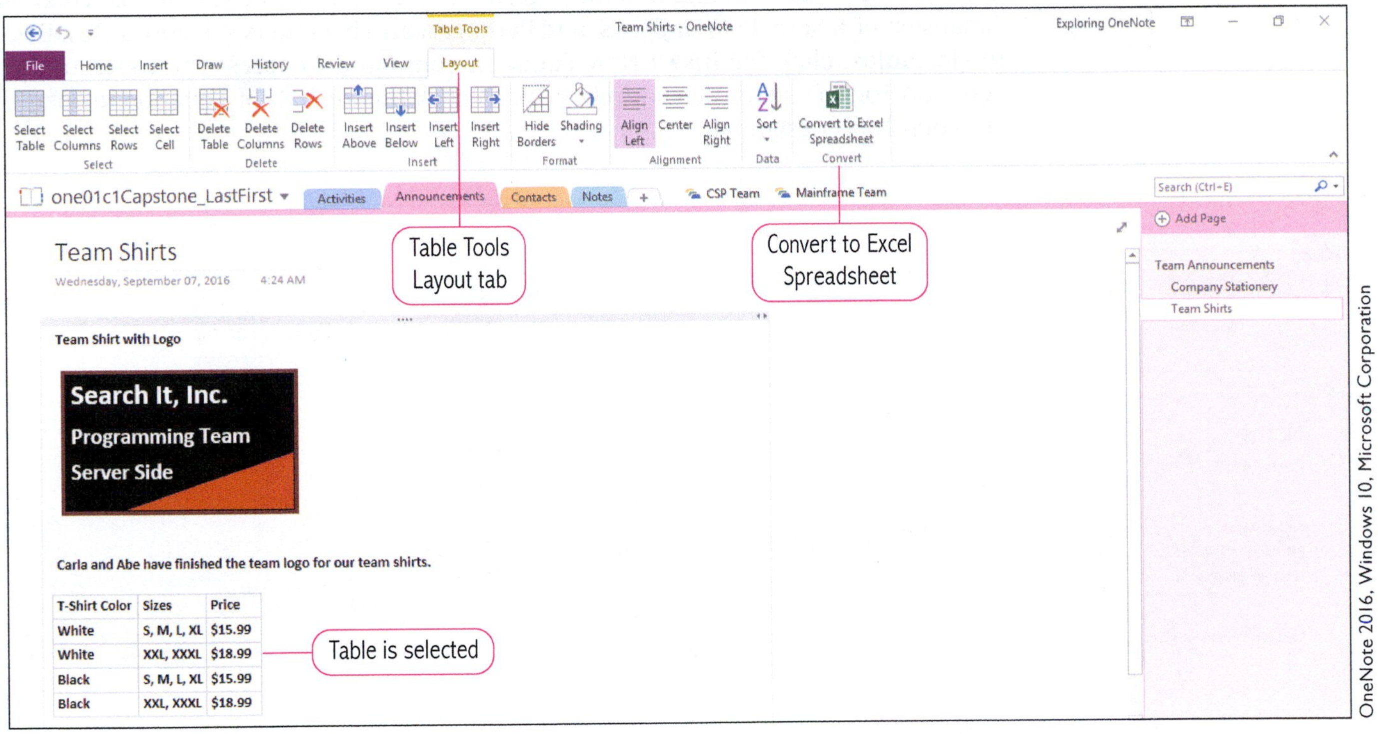

FIGURE 1.32 Convert OneNote Table to an Excel Spreadsheet

Add a Calculation

There may be times in your note taking that you will need to add a calculation. Whereas you could open a calculator app, it is not necessary. OneNote enables you to type calculations directly on your page.

To add a calculation, complete the following steps:

1. Click on the page where you want to add the calculation.
2. Type the calculation, ending it with an equal sign (=).
3. Press Enter.

Table 1.2 shows the standard math symbols used in Microsoft OneNote 2016 for mathematic operators.

TABLE 1.2	Math Symbols	
*		Multiplication
/		Division
−		Subtraction
+		Addition
^		Exponentiation (to the power of)
( )		Parentheses are used to group values in equations

Pearson Education, Inc.

Example: (2 * 8) + (3 − 2) + 23 =

When this example is keyed into OneNote, the application automatically calculates the answer to be 40. For more complex calculations, click on the Insert tab, and in the Symbols group, click the Equation arrow to display common mathematical formulas available for inserting into the page, including Area of Circle, Binomial Theorem, Expansion of a Sum, Fourier Series, and Pythagorean Theorem (see Figure 1.33). Below the formulas, click the Insert New Equation command to access the contextual tab Equation Tools Design. Alternatively, you can click the top half of Equation to open the Equation Tools Design tab.

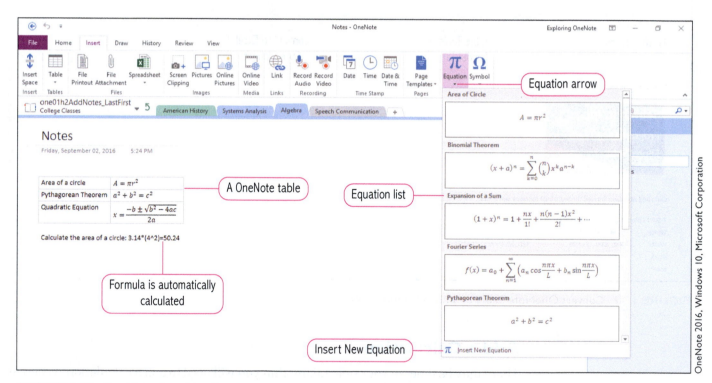

FIGURE 1.33   OneNote Calculates Equations

Integrate Office Files

STEP 6   ▶▶   Most Microsoft applications can be integrated with each other, and OneNote is no exception. As previously noted, using the Insert tab, you can attach files. You can also use the Insert tab to insert a file printout. This "prints" the document into your notebook. This can be helpful when your instructor sends you a file with information you would like to incorporate directly into your notes. To insert a file printout, open the page where you want the file printout inserted, click to place the pointer in the page where you want the file inserted, and then click File Printout in the Files group on the Insert tab. Navigate to your storage media, select the file, and then click Insert. The file will be "printed" to the OneNote page (see Figure 1.34). This can be done with Word, Excel, and PowerPoint files.

The Spreadsheet command in the Files group enables you to include an existing spreadsheet or to create a new Excel spreadsheet. While you are able to create a table and even convert an existing table into an Excel spreadsheet, there will be occasions when you may need to incorporate a more complex or currently existing spreadsheet into your notebook, rather than creating it from scratch (see Figure 1.34). For instance, your instructor may email you an Excel spreadsheet with the grading rubric for your course.

To insert an existing Excel Spreadsheet, complete the following steps:

1. Click the Spreadsheet arrow in the Files group on the Insert tab.
2. Click Existing Excel Spreadsheet.
3. Navigate to your student data files, select the Excel file, and then click Insert.
4. Select one of the three options in the Insert File dialog box: Attach File, Insert Spreadsheet, or Insert a Chart or Table.

To create a new spreadsheet, complete the following steps:

1. Click the Spreadsheet arrow in the Files group on the Insert tab.
2. Click New Excel Spreadsheet.
3. Click the Edit button in the spreadsheet window to open Excel.
4. Create the spreadsheet and close the Excel application.

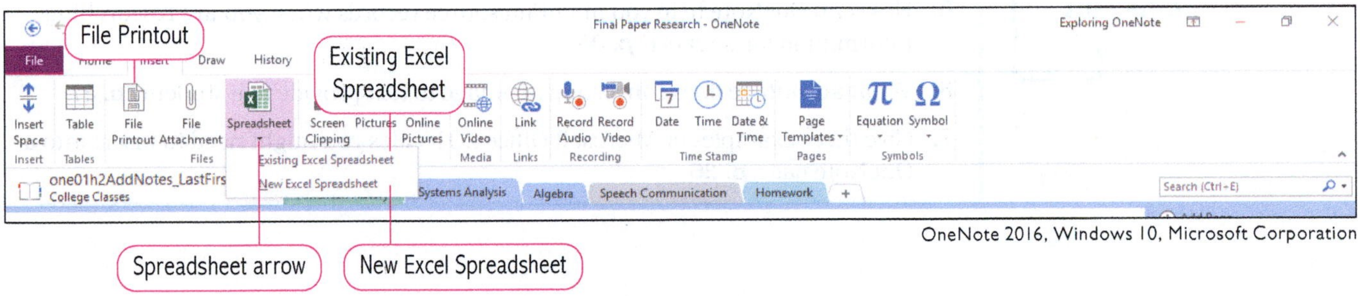

FIGURE 1.34 Existing Excel Spreadsheet and New Excel Spreadsheet Commands

Another way to add content from any Microsoft application is to use the Print command, very much the same as you would Print to paper. Instead of using the default printer to print the file to, select Send to OneNote, as shown in Figure 1.35. In this way, you can add content to OneNote without opening the OneNote application.

To use the Print command to add content, complete the following steps:

1. Click the File tab in any Microsoft Office application, click Print, and then to the left of the printer name, click the arrow.
2. Scroll to locate Send to OneNote 2016 and select it.
3. Click Print on the Print screen.
4. Select the notebook, the section, and the page to which you want to print the file in the Select Location in OneNote dialog box.
5. Click OK.

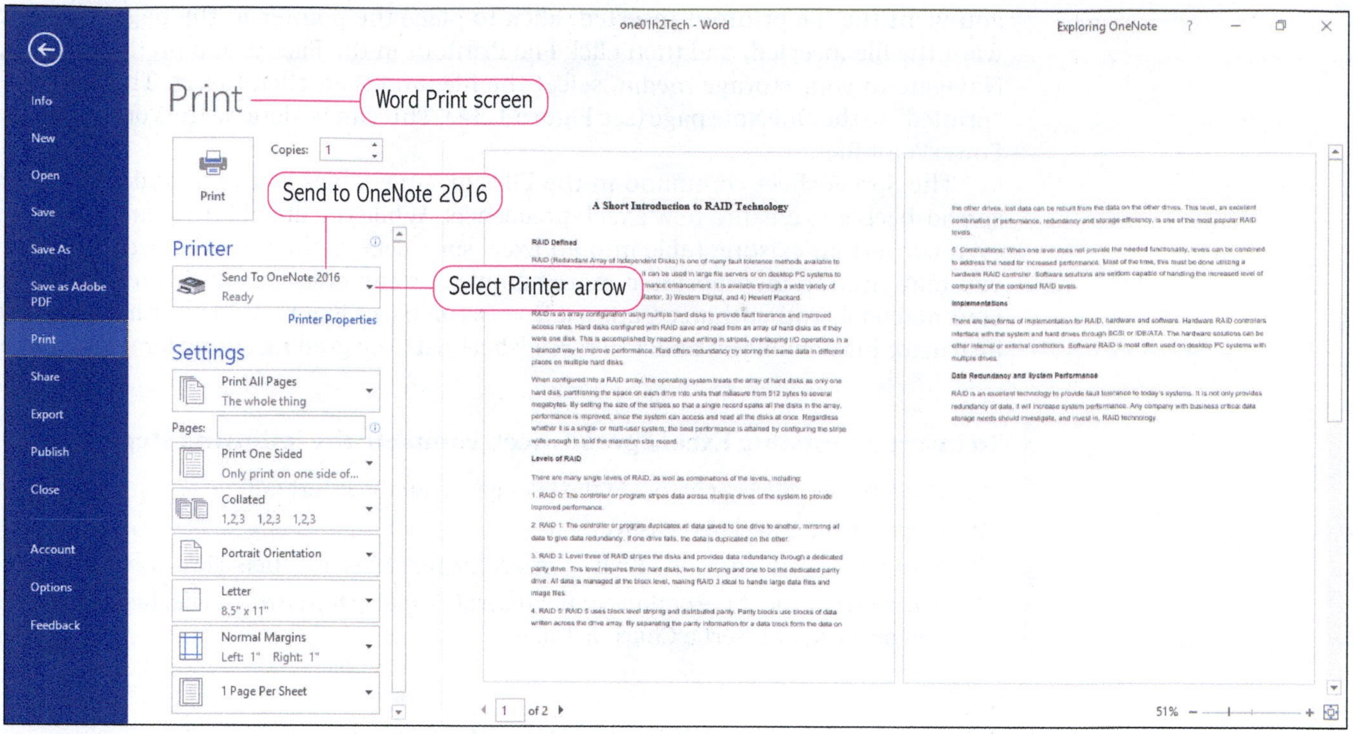

FIGURE 1.35 Print Files into OneNote

Word 2016, Windows 10, Microsoft Corporation

The OneNote page the file printed will display the file printout. At this point, you can move or copy the page to any section.

Quick Concepts

5. How can OneNote help you maintain source records when you are researching information for a report? *p. 30*

6. What advantage does converting an image to text provide to a student? *p. 31*

7. Give three examples of Microsoft Office 2016 files you might need to insert into a OneNote page. *p. 36*

Hands-On Exercises

Skills covered: Add Notes • Create Screen Clips • Use New Quick Note Tool • Insert a Photo • Insert Links • Convert Text from an Image • Attach a File • Create a Table • Convert a Table to Excel • Add a Calculation • Insert File Printouts • Create a New Excel Spreadsheet • Use Print to Add Content

2 OneNote 2016 Content

Now that Bonnie's notebook is set up, you will help her add notes, screen clips, a link, and an illustration. Bonnie has a photo of the notes her professor projected on the class whiteboard. A classmate told her the notes photo can be converted into text in OneNote. She has asked you to help her with the conversion. She also needs to attach and embed additional files her instructor provided. Bonnie is having difficulty learning the Algebra formulas, and has asked for help creating a table of the formulas and an example of a calculation.

STEP 1 » ADD NOTES AND ATTACH A FILE

Bonnie needs to add team project information, and screenshots to her class notebook. You will help her add notes to the notebook created in Hands-On Exercise 1. Refer to Figure 1.36 as you complete Step 1.

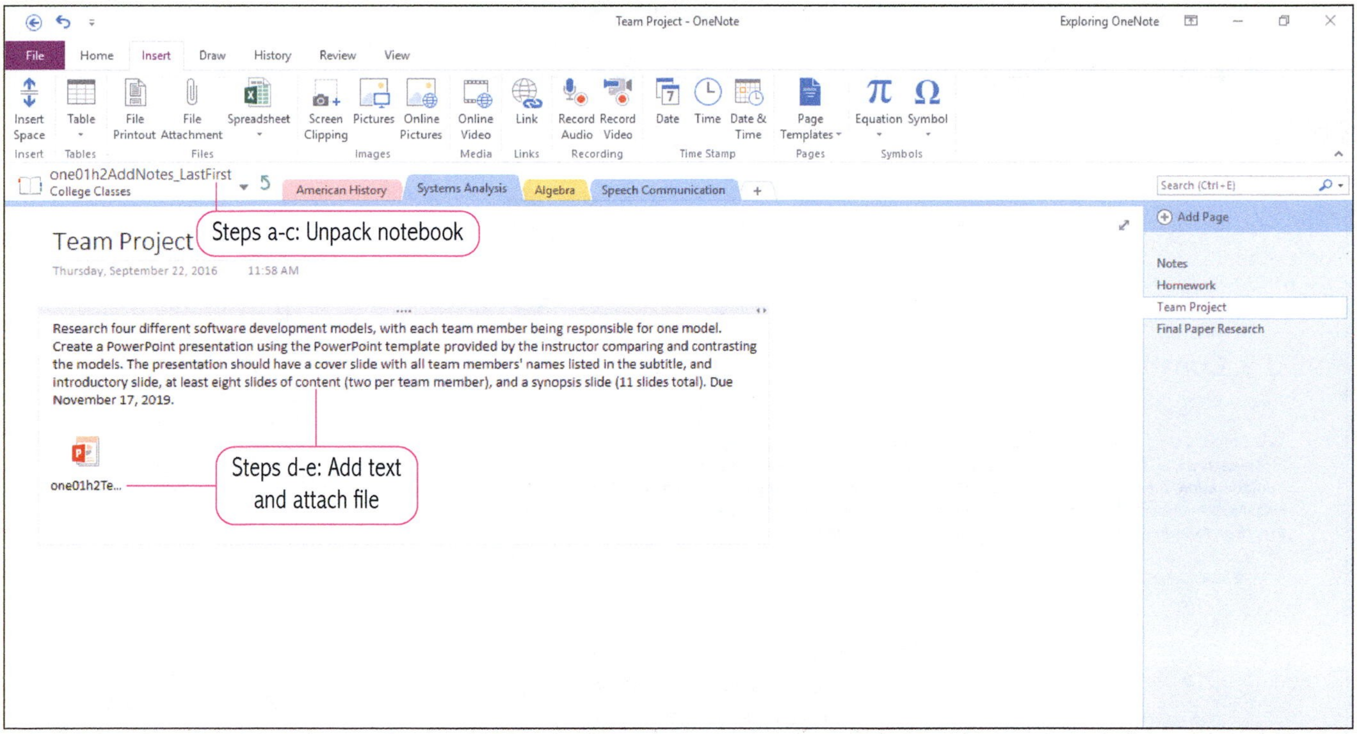

OneNote 2016, Windows 10, Microsoft Corporation

FIGURE 1.36 An Attached File

a. Open one01h1ClassNotes_LastFirst if you closed it at the end of Hands-On Exercise 1.

b. Click the **File tab**, click **Export**, click **Notebook**, select **OneNote Package (*.onepkg)**, verify the location the file is exported to is your storage device, and then click **Export**. Change the file name to **one01h2AddNotes_LastFirst**. Navigate to your storage device, and click **Save** to export one01h1ClassNotes_LastFirst as **one01h2AddNotes_LastFirst**.

c. Navigate to the location to which you exported the notebook. Double-click on **one01h2AddNotes_LastFirst** to unpack the notebook. Verify the name of the notebook in the Unpack Notebook dialog box. Verify the path to your storage device. Click **Create**.

d. Click the **College Classes section group icon**, and click on the **Systems Analysis section tab**. Click the **Team Project Page tab**. Click below the title, and then type the following:

> **Research four different software development models, with each team member being responsible for one model. Create a PowerPoint presentation using the PowerPoint template provided by the instructor comparing and contrasting the models. The presentation should have a cover slide with all team members' names listed in the subtitle, an introductory slide, at least eight slides of content (two per team member), and a synopsis slide (11 slides total). Due November 17, 2019.**

> Press **Enter** twice.

e. Click the **Insert tab**, and click **File Attachment** in the Files group. Navigate to your student data files. Select *one01h2Template.potx* and click **Insert**. Click **Attach File**.

STEP 2 ›› **USE THE NEW QUICK NOTE TOOL AND INSERT A LINK**

Bonnie needs to add research information for her American History research project to her notebook. In this section, you will help her add a URL link to the Final Paper Research page and add information from the Internet. Her instructor also suggested she locate images of the Declaration of Independence and the U.S. Constitution to use in her final paper. Refer to Figures 1.37 and 1.38 as you complete Step 2.

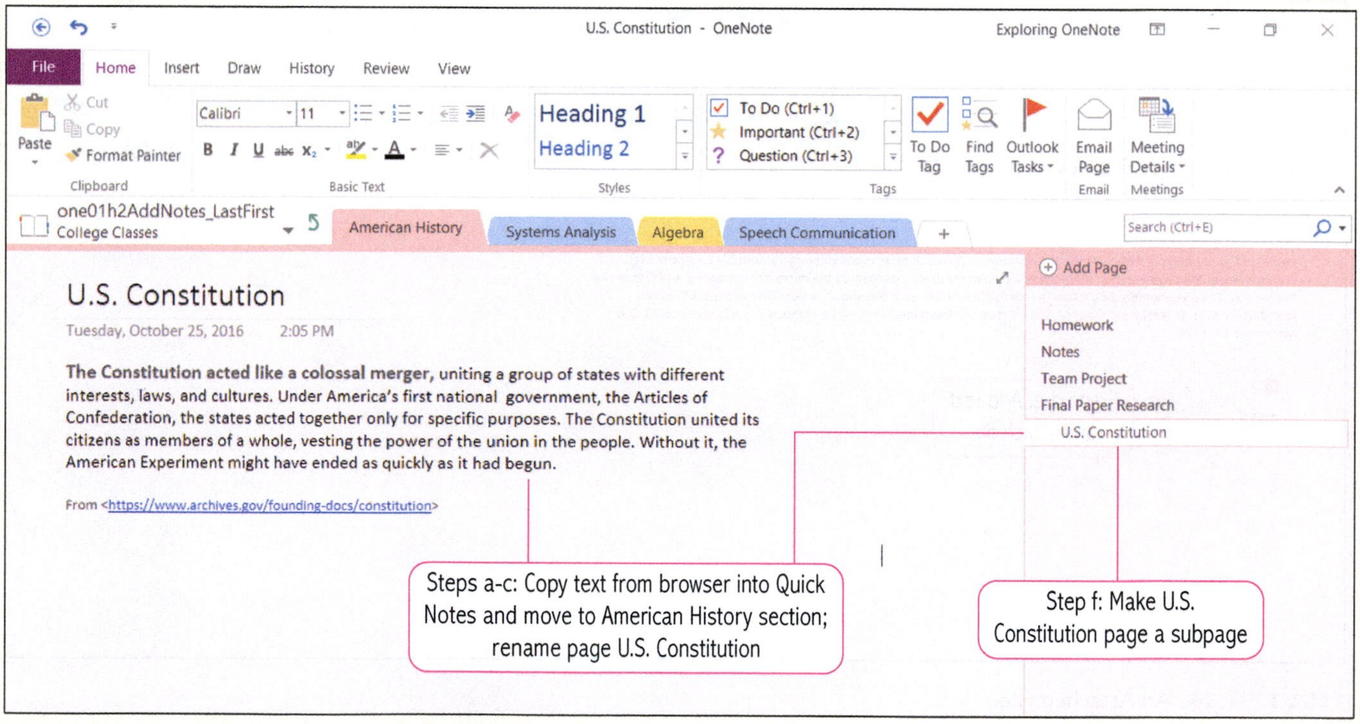

FIGURE 1.37 Capture Content with the Quick Note Tool

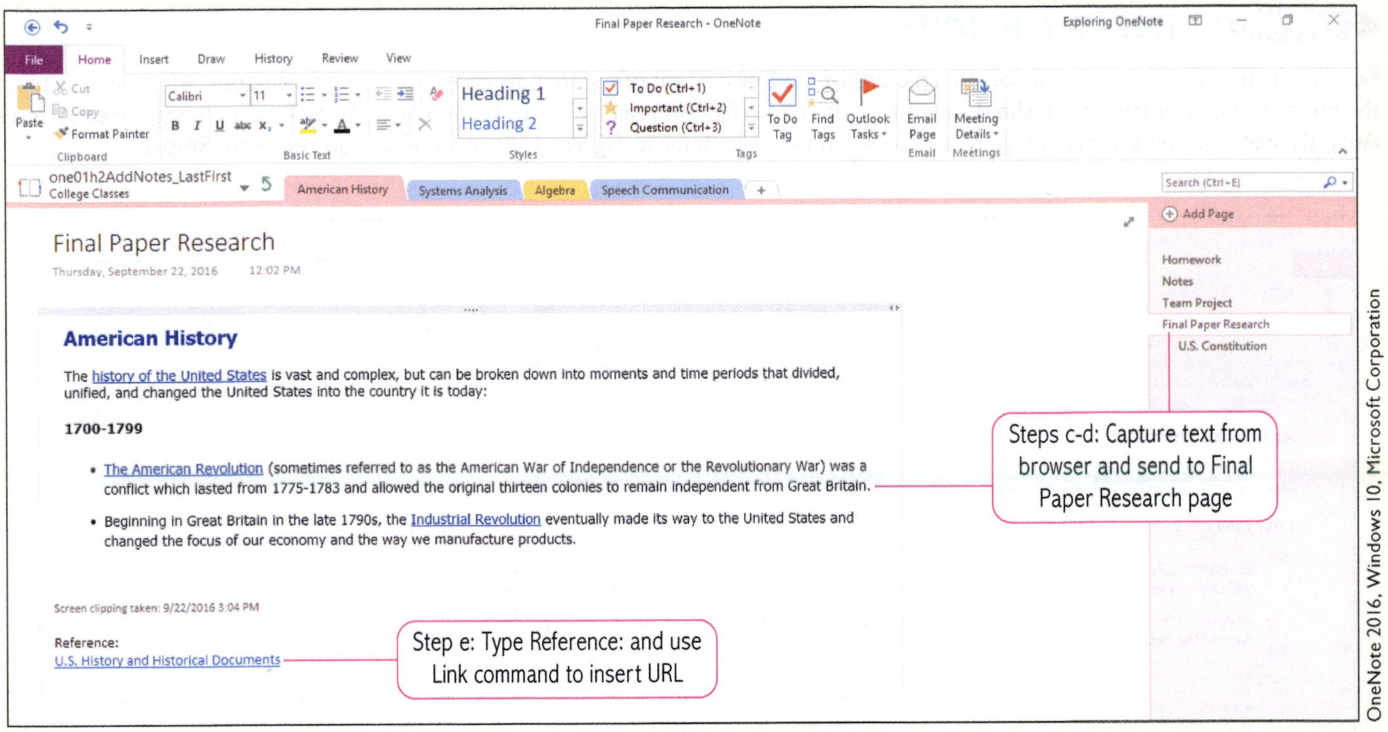

The figure shows a OneNote 2016 window with the following content:

Final Paper Research
Thursday, September 22, 2016   12:02 PM

American History

The history of the United States is vast and complex, but can be broken down into moments and time periods that divided, unified, and changed the United States into the country it is today:

1700-1799

- The American Revolution (sometimes referred to as the American War of Independence or the Revolutionary War) was a conflict which lasted from 1775-1783 and allowed the original thirteen colonies to remain independent from Great Britain.

- Beginning in Great Britain in the late 1790s, the Industrial Revolution eventually made its way to the United States and changed the focus of our economy and the way we manufacture products.

Screen clipping taken: 9/22/2016 3:04 PM

Reference:
U.S. History and Historical Documents

Callout: Steps c-d: Capture text from browser and send to Final Paper Research page

Callout: Step e: Type Reference: and use Link command to insert URL

FIGURE 1.38 Content Captured with Windows+Shift+S

a. Open your browser, and navigate to **https://www.archives.gov/founding-docs/constitution**. Select the **paragraph** beginning *The Constitution acted like a colossal merger, uniting a group of states with different interests, laws, and cultures.* Press **Ctrl+C** to copy the selected text. Open the Show hidden icons tray. Click the **New quick note icon**. Ensure the pointer is in the Quick Notes window. Press **Ctrl+V** to paste the copied text into the Quick Notes window. Close the Quick Notes window. Return to OneNote. Click the **green return arrow** to return to the main notebook. Click the **Navigation pane arrow**. Select **Quick Notes**.

b. Right-click on the **Quick Notes page** you just created, and click **Move or Copy**. Expand the **one01h2AddNotes_LastFirst** notebook, expand the **College Classes section group,** select the **American History** section, and then click **Move**.

c. Select **one01h2AddNotes_LastFirst** in the Navigation Pane, Click the **College Classes section group tab**, click the **American History section tab**, and then verify the page moved to the American History section of your notebook. Rename the page as **U.S. Constitution**.

d. Click the **Final Paper Research Page tab** in the same section. Maximize your browser and navigate to **https://www.usa.gov/history#item-36822**. Scroll down the page until you see the heading American History. Press **Windows+Shift+S** and select the title *American History* and all of the *1700–1799* section. Expand **one01h2AddNotes_LastFirst** in the Select Location in OneNote dialog box. Expand the **College Classes section group**. Select the **American History section**, expanding notebook and sections as needed. Select the **Final Paper Research page**, and click **Send to Selected Location**.

e. Click below the screen shot in OneNote 2016, and press **Enter** twice. Type **Reference:** below the screen shot. Click **Link** in the Links group on the Insert tab. Type **U.S. History and Historical Documents** in the Text to display text box. Type **https://www.usa.gov/history#item-36822** in the Address text box. Click **OK**, and press **Enter**.

f. Right-click on the **U.S. Constitution page tab**, and click **Make Subpage**.

STEP 3 » INSERT PHOTOS

Bonnie's instructor suggested she locate a picture of the Declaration of Independence to use in her final paper. After downloading the image to her storage media, she decided to paste it into her American History section Final Paper Research page. Her Systems Analysis professor sent her an image to add to her notebook. Refer to Figures 1.39 and 1.40 as you complete Step 3.

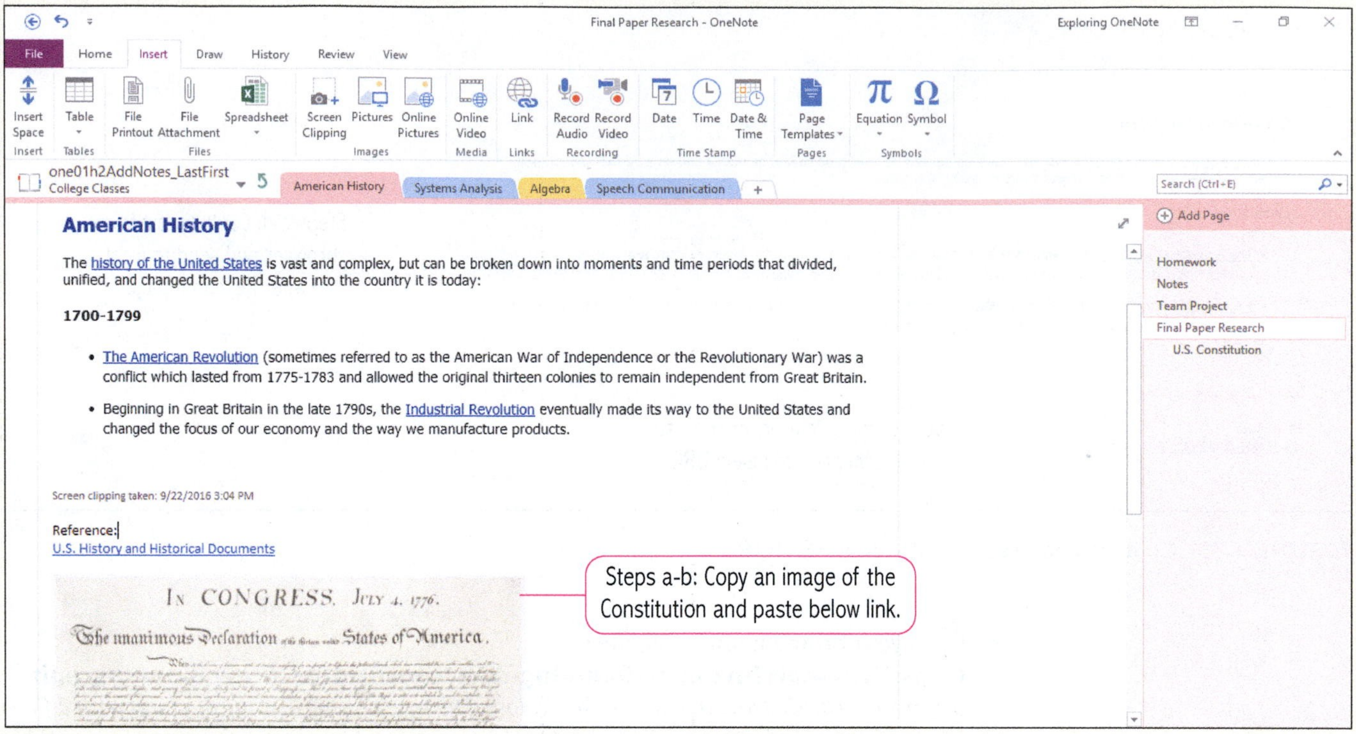

OneNote 2016, Windows 10, Microsoft Corporation

FIGURE 1.39 Website Photo Copied and Pasted into OneNote

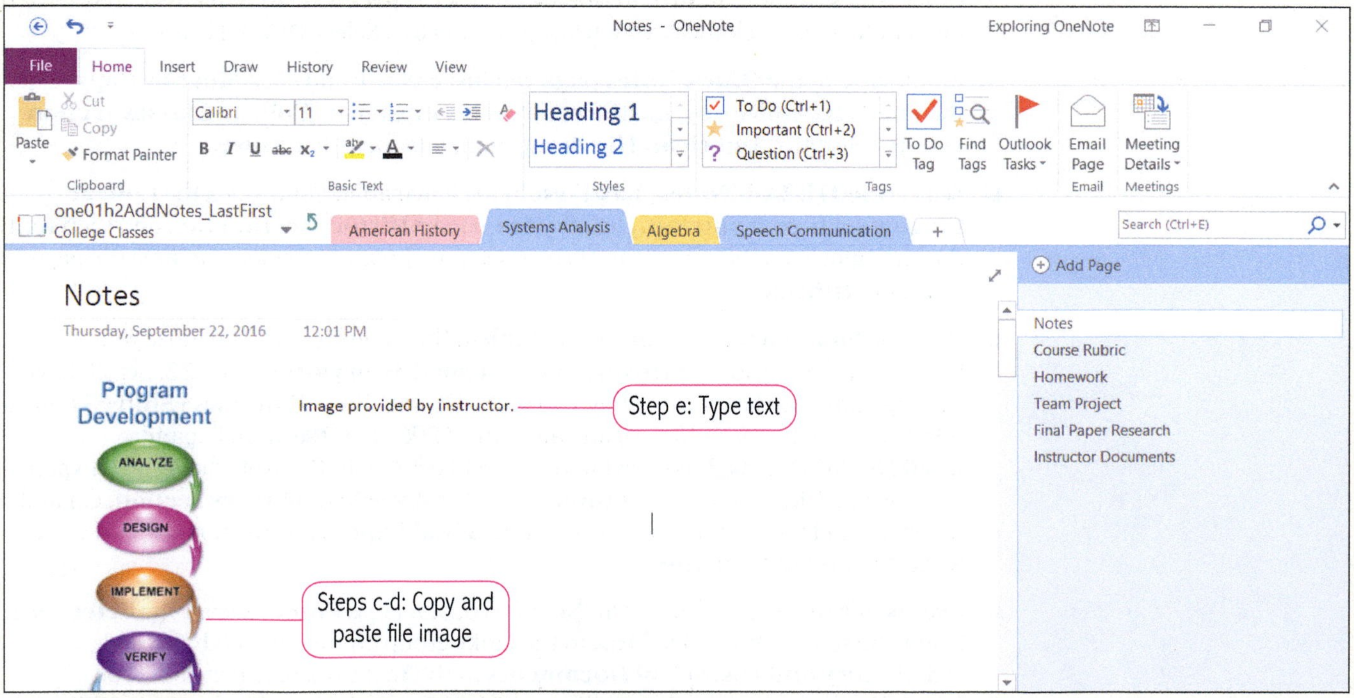

OneNote 2016, Windows 10, Microsoft Corporation

FIGURE 1.40 Paste a File into a Page

a. Click the **Final Paper Research page tab** in the American History section below the previously inserted information.

b. Return to the browser. Click **Declaration of Independence** in the *What's on This Page* box. Right-click on the **image** of the Declaration of Independence. **Copy** the image. Navigate to the American History section **Final Paper Research page**. Press **Ctrl+V** to paste the image in the Final Paper Research page below the U.S. History and Historical Documents link.

c. Click the **Systems Analysis section tab**. Click the **Notes page tab**. Click **File Explorer** on your taskbar. Navigate to your student data files. Click the **View tab**. Click **Large icons** in the Layout group. Right-click the *one01h2Development.jpg* image. Click **Copy**. Close the File Explorer window.

d. Click below the date on the Notes page. Press **Ctrl+V** to paste the image.

e. Click the **page** to the right of Program Development, and type **Image provided by instructor.**

STEP 4 ▶▶ **CONVERT TEXT FROM AN IMAGE AND ATTACH A FILE**

Bonnie was not able to attend the last Systems Analysis and Design Methods class. Her friend took a picture of the notes the instructor projected onto the whiteboard, and then sent her the image by email. Bonnie would like to add some information to the notes. Because annotating the image is difficult, she has decided to convert the image contents to text. Bonnie's instructor sent a document and a PowerPoint template to the class. Bonnie would also like to attach the files to her notebook. Refer to Figures 1.41 and 1.42 as you complete Step 4.

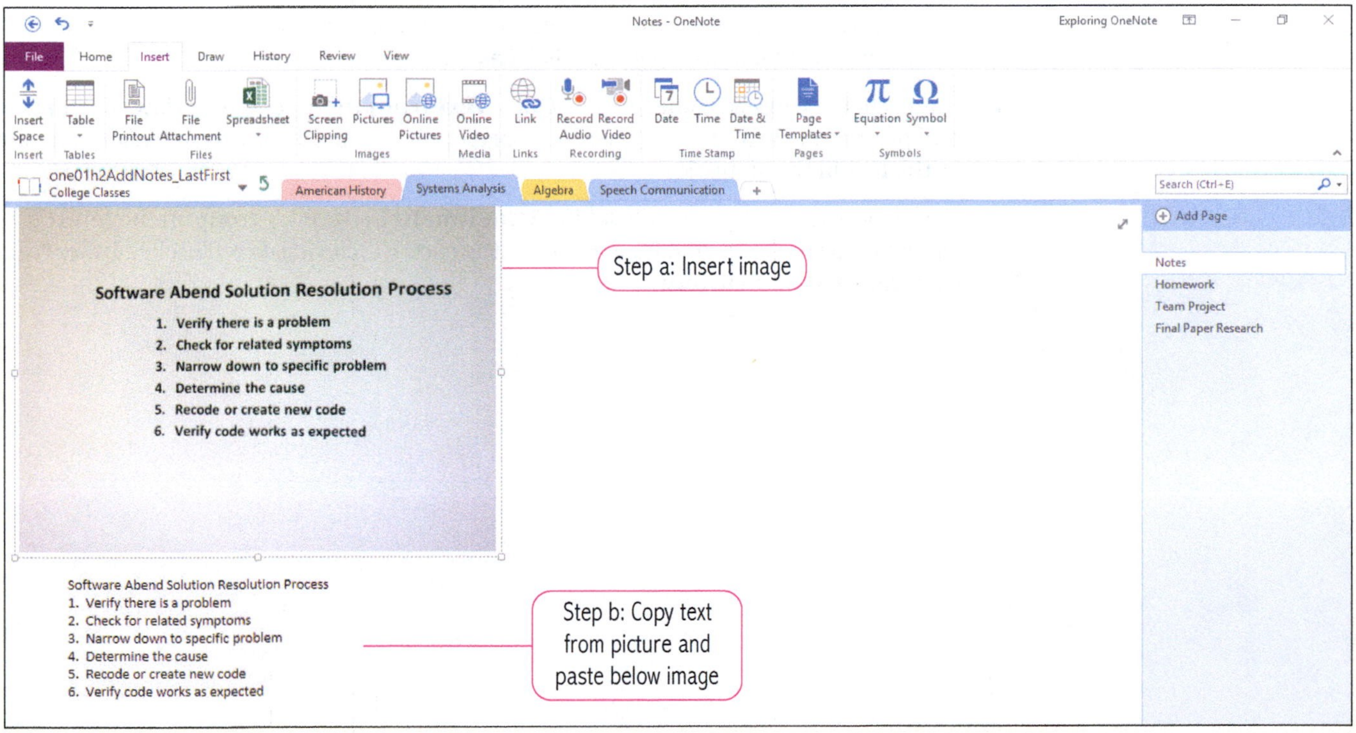

FIGURE 1.41 Text Copied from an Image

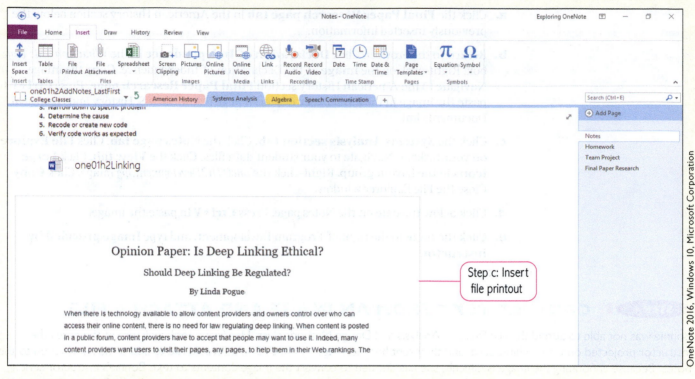

FIGURE 1.42 The File Printout Command

    a. Click below the program development image on the Systems Analysis section Notes page. Click **Pictures** in the Images group on the Insert tab. Navigate to your student data files. Select *one01h2Whiteboard.jpg*, and click **Insert**.

    b. Right-click the inserted image. Click **Copy Text from Picture**. Click below the image, and press **Ctrl+V**. Make any necessary corrections to the pasted text to make it the same as the text in the image.

    c. Click below the pasted text. Click **File Attachment** in the Files group on the Insert tab. Navigate to your student data files. Select the *one01h2Linking.docx* file, click **Insert**, and then click **Insert Printout**.

STEP 5 » CREATE A TABLE AND ADD A CALCULATION

Bonnie's Algebra homework requires her to use the formulas for the area of a circle, the Pythagorean theorem, and the Quadratic Equation. To help her remember these formulas, she will add them to her Algebra Notes page, and then use OneNote to calculate the area of a circle. She will also add a page with a grades table. Refer to Figures 1.43 and 1.44 as you complete Step 5.

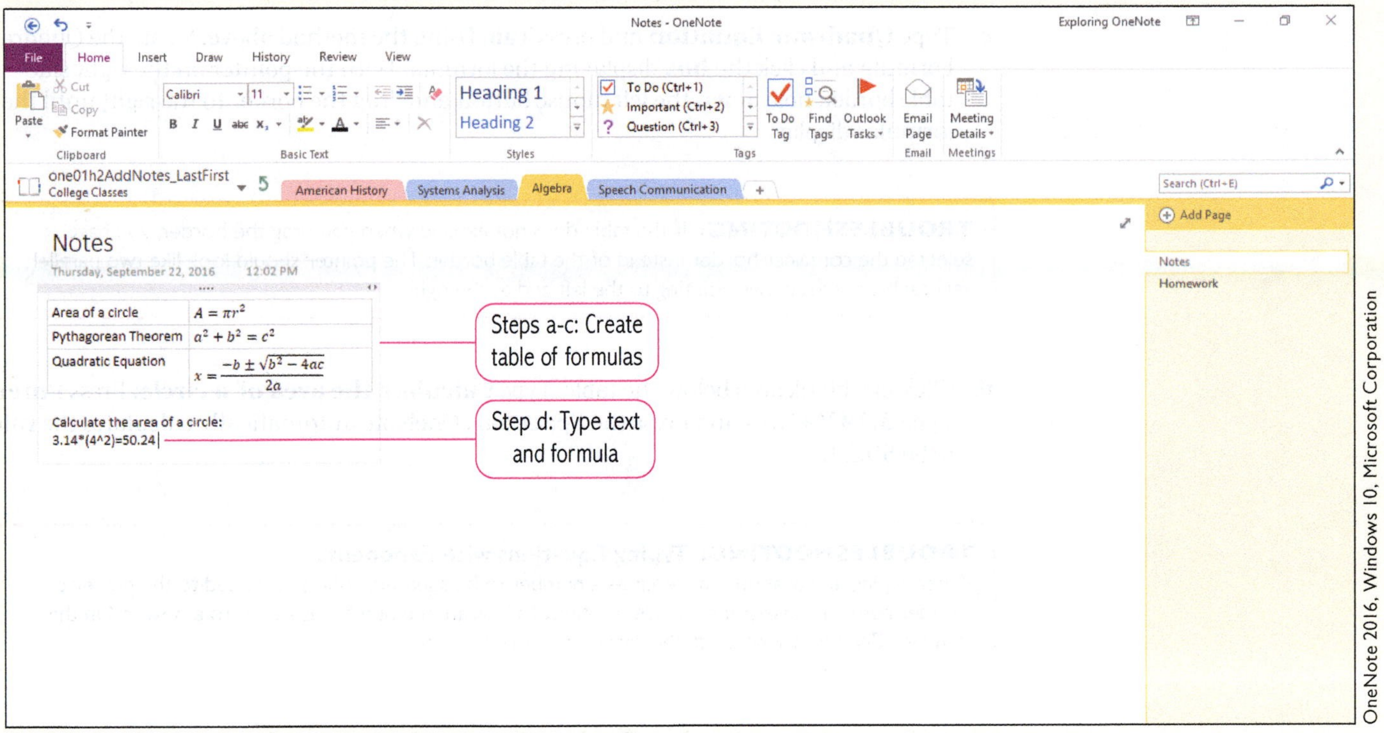

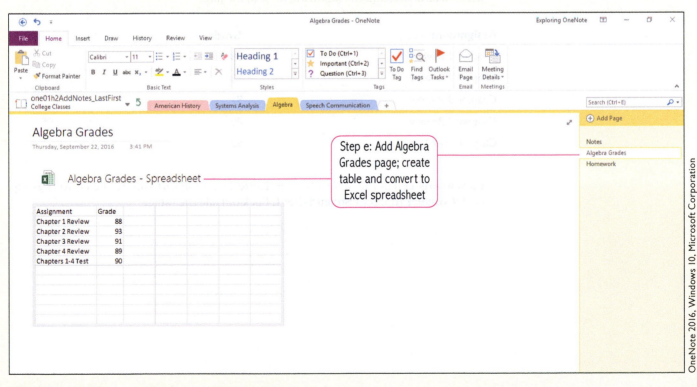

FIGURE 1.43 Equation Formulas in OneNote

FIGURE 1.44 Convert a Table to an Excel Spreadsheet

a. Click below the date on the Algebra section Notes page, and type **Area of a circle**. Press **Tab**. Click the **Insert tab**, and click the **Equation arrow** in the Symbols group. Click the **box** that displays the Area of Circle formula. Press **Enter**.

b. Type **Pythagorean Theorem** and press **Tab**. Click the **Insert tab**, and click the **Equation arrow** in the Symbols group. Scroll to locate the Pythagorean Theorem. Click the **box** that displays the Pythagorean Theorem formula, and press **Enter**.

c. Type **Quadratic Equation** and press **Tab**. Using the method above, locate the Quadratic Formula and click the **box** displaying the formula. With the pointer on the right side table border, hold down the left mouse button and drag the border to the right until the formulas display.

TROUBLESHOOTING: If the table does not expand when you drag the border, you have selected the container border instead of the table border. The pointer should look like two parallel vertical bars with arrows pointing to the left and to the right.

---

d. Click in a blank area below the table. Type **Calculate the area of a circle:** Press **Enter**. Type **3.14*(4^2)=** and press the **Spacebar**. OneNote automatically calculates the value to be 50.24.

TROUBLESHOOTING: Typing Equations with Exponents
When typing an equation that requires a number to be squared, cubed, or raised to the power of another number (an exponent), use the caret to indicate the number is raised to a power. On the standard QWERTY keyboard, the caret is the Shift+6 or ^.

---

e. Add a page named **Algebra Grades**. Move the **Algebra Grades** page below the Algebra section Notes page. Click below the date on the Algebra Grades page. Using the same method as above, add the following table to the page:

Assignment	Grade
Chapter 1 Review	88
Chapter 2 Review	93
Chapter 3 Review	91
Chapter 4 Review	89
Chapters 1-4 Test	90

f. Click in **any cell** in the table. Click the **Table Tools Layout tab**. In the Convert group, click **Convert to Excel Spreadsheet**. Click outside the table.

STEP 6 » INTEGRATE OFFICE FILES

Bonnie's instructor emailed a document to review for homework and a spreadsheet that breaks down course grade points. After opening and reviewing the files, Bonnie has decided to add them to her notebook. For convenience, Bonnie has decided to add a class schedule to the notebook, too. Refer to Figures 1.45–1.47 as you complete Step 6.

OneNote 2016, Windows 10, Microsoft Corporation

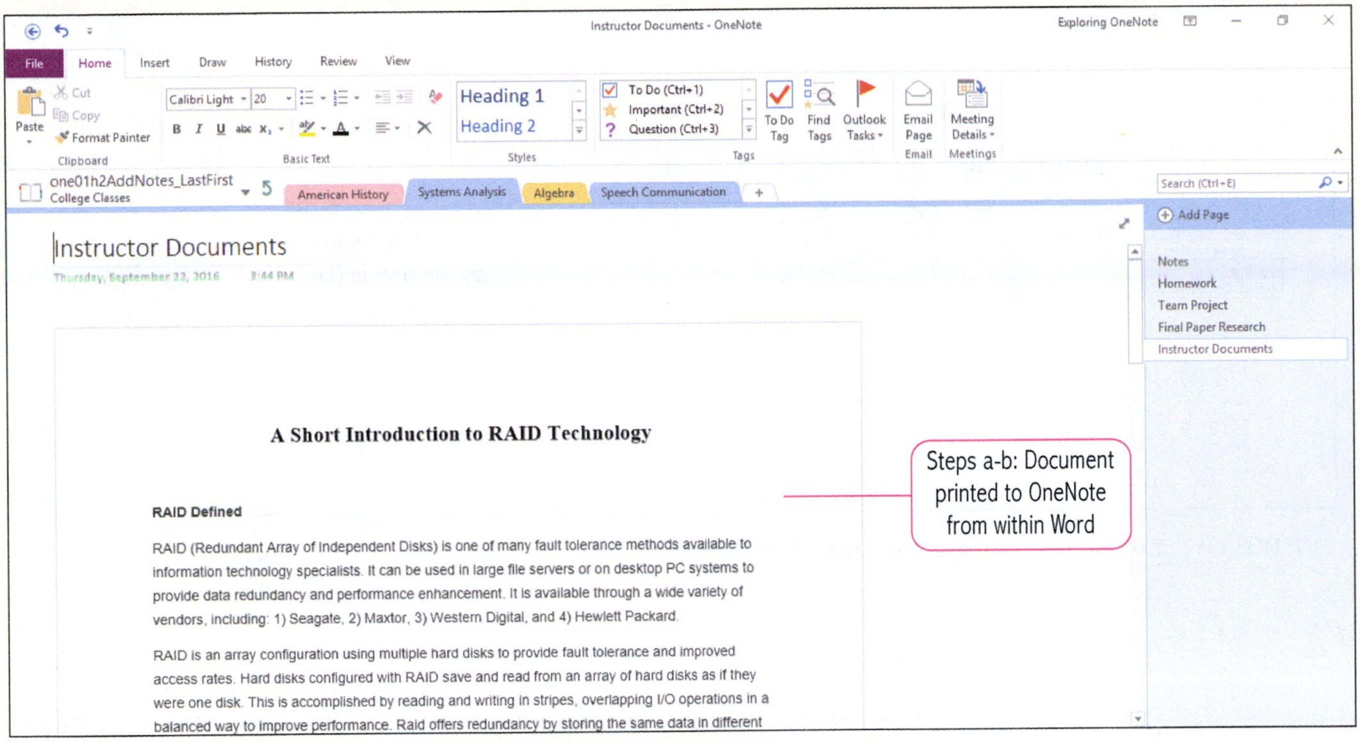

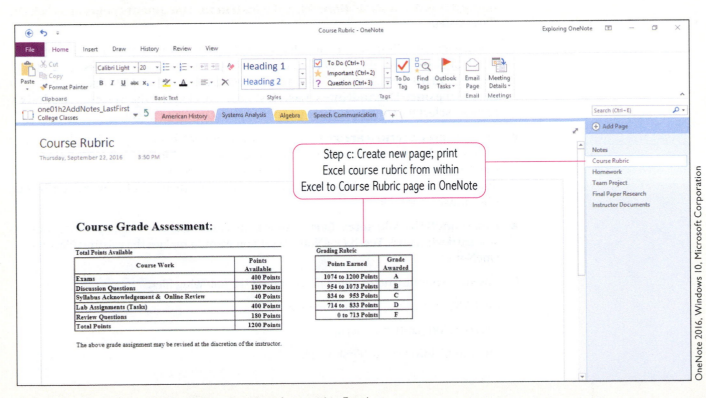

FIGURE 1.45 Document Printed to OneNote from within Word

OneNote 2016, Windows 10, Microsoft Corporation

FIGURE 1.46 Spreadsheet Printed to OneNote from within Excel

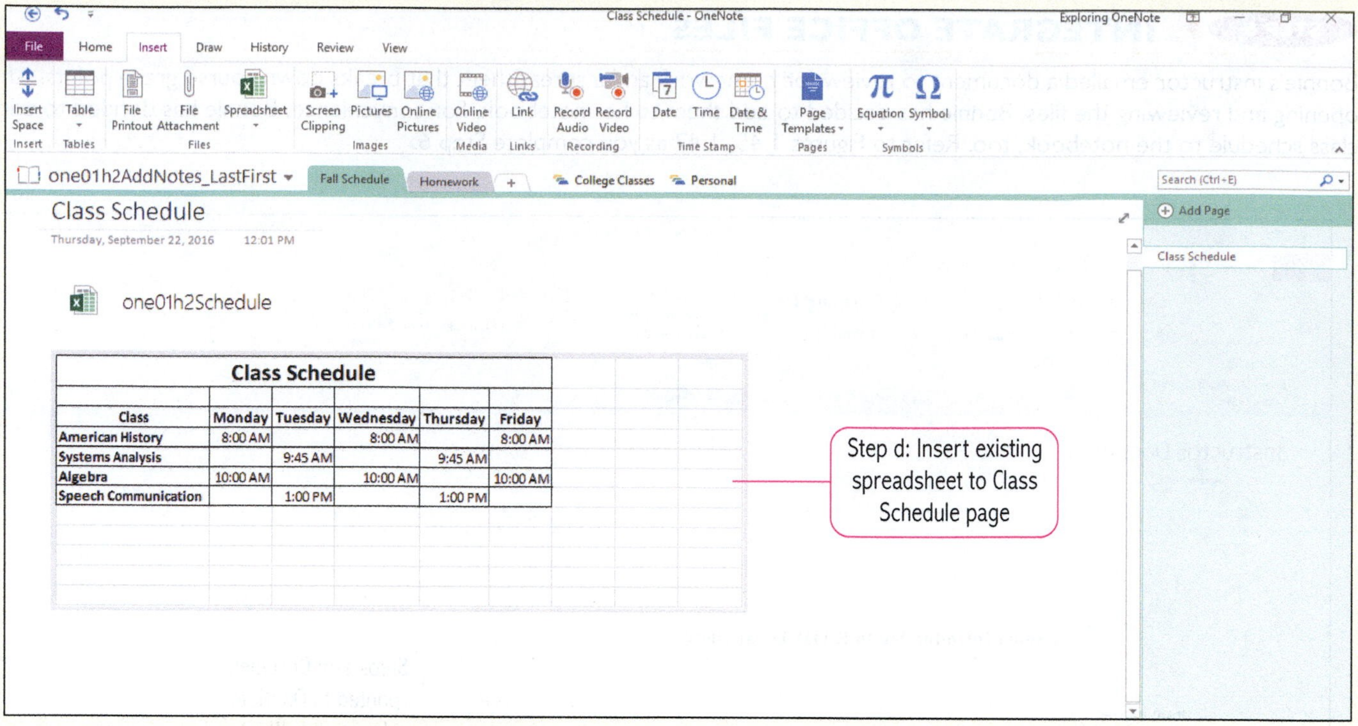

OneNote 2016, Windows 10, Microsoft Corporation

FIGURE 1.47 Existing Excel Spreadsheet Inserted into OneNote

a. Click the **Systems Analysis section**, add a page, and title it **Instructor Documents**, and press **Enter**. In Word 2016, open *one01h2Tech.docx* and enable editing. Click the **File tab**, and click **Print**. Change the printer to **Send to OneNote 2016**. Click **Print**.

b. Return to OneNote. Expand the **one01h2AddNotes_LastFirst notebook** in the Select Location in OneNote dialog box. Expand the **College Classes group section**. Expand the **Systems Analysis section**. Select the **Instructor Documents page**, and click **OK**. Close **Word**.

c. Add a page titled **Course Rubric** below the Notes page. Open *one01h2Rubric.xlsx* in Excel. Click the **File tab**. Click **Print**. Change the printer to **Send to OneNote 2016**, and click **Print**. Return to OneNote. In the Select Location in OneNote dialog box, expand the **one01h2AddNotes_LastFirst** notebook. Expand the **Systems Analysis** section. Select the **Course Rubric page**, and click **OK**. Close **Excel**.

d. Click the **green return arrow** to return to the main notebook. Click below the title of the Class Schedule page in the Fall Schedule section. Click the **Spreadsheet arrow** in the Files group on the Insert tab. Select **Existing Excel Spreadsheet**, navigate to your data files, select *one01h2Schedule.xlsx*, click **Insert**, and then click **Insert Spreadsheet**. Click outside the table.

e. Export **one01h2AddNotes_LastFirst** as a OneNote Package (*.onepkg) file to your storage device. Click **Yes**, if OneNote asks if you want to replace the existing file. Close OneNote.

f. Based on your instructor's directions, submit the following files:

one01h1ClassNotes_LastFirst.onepkg

one01h1Jon_LastFirst.onepkg

one01h2AddNotes_LastFirst.onepkg

Chapter Objectives Review

After reading this chapter, you have accomplished the following objectives:

1. **Create and manage notebooks.**
   - Discover the OneNote 2016 interface: While similar to other Microsoft Office Applications, there are some differences in the OneNote Ribbon. The interface includes the Quick Access Toolbar, the Ribbon, the Notebook Pane, Section tabs, Search box, Page tabs, and the Page area.
   - Create a notebook and add sections and pages: Using sections, you can customize a notebook to include all you need in one notebook, or create a notebook for each area of your life.
   - Group notebook sections: Grouping sections of a notebook makes it easier to keep information that goes together in one location.
   - Rename and delete sections and pages: As your needs change, you can add, rename, or delete sections and pages.
   - Copy or move a section or page to another notebook: You can save time by copying or moving a notebook page or section to another notebook.
   - Rearrange sections and pages, and merge sections: After you have created a notebook, you may need to rearrange sections or pages. You may find that some information spread through two or more sections needs to be in one section. Merging sections corrects this problem.
   - Save, print, and print preview a notebook: OneNote automatically saves content added to it. In OneNote, you can only print a section or page. To print the entire notebook, you would have to print each section separately.
   - Send notes from OneNote using Outlook: Using Outlook or another email provider, you can send sections of your notebook to a colleague or team member.
   - Export a notebook: Because OneNote automatically saves to the location where the notebook was originally created, to make a backup or copy of the notebook, you must export the notebook.
   - Email a note to OneNote 2016: After setting up your email to work with OneNote, you can email a note to your notebook using the me@outlook.com email address.

2. **Add content to OneNote.**
   - Add notes: OneNote provides containers for you to type into to add your notes. You can click anywhere in the page area to add a container.
   - Create screen clips: You can use Windows+Shift+S to capture part or all of a screen into a screenshot.
   - Use the New quick note tool: With the New quick note tool, you can type a quick note into a Quick Notes page, then later move it to the appropriate page or section.
   - Insert a link: To insert a link, either copy and paste the URL from the address bar in your browser, or use the Link command in the Links group on the Insert tab.
   - Paste or insert a photo: To add images to your notebook, you can copy and paste an image on your screen, or insert a photo or another image file.
   - Convert text from an image: To capture text from an image, first insert or paste the image into your OneNote page, then right-click the image and click Copy Text from Picture. Click anywhere in the page area, and then paste the text into a new container.
   - Record or embed media files to a page: Audio and video recordings can be created from within OneNote. Audio recordings require a microphone. Video recordings require a webcam and microphone. Media files can be inserted or embedded into OneNote using commands in the Files, Images, Media, Links, and Recording groups on the Insert tab.
   - Attach a file or insert a file printout: To attach a file, click the Insert tab, select the appropriate command from the Files, Images, or Recording groups, navigate to the file's location, and then click either Attach File, or Insert Printout.
   - Create a table: To create a table, type the contents of the first cell, then press Tab. Type the contents of the next cell, then press the Tab key to move to the next cell. When the row is complete, press Enter to move to the next row of the table.
   - Convert a table to Excel: When you need more functionality than the tables in OneNote allow, the Convert to Excel Spreadsheet command converts the OneNote table into an embedded and editable Excel spreadsheet file. In this file, you can create charts, insert complicated formulas, add conditional formatting, and more.
   - Add a calculation: OneNote will calculate values for you. Type the equation using the math symbols *, /, -, +, ^, and (). After the equation is typed, press the = key and then press Space.
   - Integrate Office files: Use the Insert tab, Files group commands to insert, attach, or print Microsoft Office Files into OneNote. Create a new Excel spreadsheet from within OneNote using the Spreadsheet button in the Files group of the Insert tab. Use the Print command in Word, Excel, or PowerPoint to print a file to a OneNote page.

Key Terms Matching

For each question, locate the term that best completes the sentence. Write the letter of the correct term in the blank:

a. Container
b. Export
c. Merge
d. Notebook
e. Notebook Pane
f. OneNote 2016
g. Page
h. Page Pane
i. Path
j. Quick Access Toolbar

k. Quick Note
l. Ribbon
m. Scope
n. Screenshot
o. Search box
p. Section
q. Section group
r. Section tab
s. Share
t. Subpage

1. _____ A file created by OneNote to hold content divided into sections and pages. *p. 4*

2. _____ This command is used to save a OneNote notebook package file to another location. *p. 15*

3. _____ A note that has not been placed into a specific page. *p. 8*

4. _____ Microsoft's most recent note taking software for laptops and desktop computers. *p. 4*

5. _____ An image created from the content displayed on your monitor. *p. 27*

6. _____ A tool that enables you to find specific types of information in a notebook, section, or page. *p. 8*

7. _____ The primary division in a notebook. *p. 4*

8. _____ A function that enables you to give others access to your OneNote notebook. *p. 9*

9. _____ Contains three command buttons: Back, Undo, and Customize Quick Access Toolbar. *p. 7*

10. _____ A feature that makes it possible to navigate from one notebook section to another. *p. 8*

11. _____ A notebook page that is indented below a previous page. *p. 8*

12. _____ An organizational tab that keeps related content together. *p. 8*

13. _____ The exact route a computer uses to find a file. *p. 16*

14. _____ Contains information inside a section. *p. 4*

15. _____ The technique used to combine the contents of two or more pages, sections, or notebooks. *p. 16*

16. _____ Contains commands used to format content, insert content, draw illustrations, set passwords, or change the view of a notebook. *p. 7*

17. _____ The area of the OneNote screen that shows page tabs for all pages included in the current selected section. *p. 8*

18. _____ Enables users to easily navigate between open notebooks. *p. 8*

19. _____ Created when you click on the OneNote page, and is used to hold text, images, or other content. *p. 27*

20. _____ Determines where OneNote looks for information for which you are searching. *p. 8*

Multiple Choice

1. What OneNote tool enables users to keep related information together?

   (a) Page group
   (b) Topic Merge
   (c) Section group
   (d) Merge tool

2. Which of the following is *not* a way to add a new page to a section?

   (a) Right-click on an existing Page tab, and click New Page
   (b) Right-click on an existing Sections tab, and click New Page
   (c) Click the Add Page command at the top of the Page Pane
   (d) Press Ctrl+N

3. Which view removes all tabs from the screen?

   (a) Full Page View
   (b) Print Layout
   (c) Dock to Desktop
   (d) Normal View

4. When using Windows+PrtScn to capture a screen clip, the image is automatically saved to the:

   (a) Image Snips folder
   (b) Screen capture folder
   (c) Screenshots folder
   (d) Image Capture folder

5. The search _____ limits the pages, sections, or notebooks searched when searching for a specific term.

   (a) Scope
   (b) Bar
   (c) Explorer
   (d) Window

6. Common math functions can be added to your notebook by:

   (a) Clicking Insert, and clicking Add Equation
   (b) Clicking Review, and clicking Add Equation
   (c) Clicking Insert, and clicking Equation
   (d) Clicking Review, and clicking Equation

7. Which of the following equations will be automatically calculated by OneNote?

   (a) $49/7 + (32*39)$ equals
   (b) $(4*35) + 67 =$
   (c) $= 29 + 32*(63/9)$
   (d) $39/3 + 42*16$

8. To make a backup of a OneNote 2016 notebook, use the:

   (a) Copy command
   (b) Save As command
   (c) Print command
   (d) Export command

9. To navigate easily to another notebook, use the _____ Pane.

   (a) Page
   (b) Notebook
   (c) Section
   (d) Password

10. All deleted pages, sections, and notebooks are moved to the:

    (a) Deletions Folder
    (b) Notebook Recycle Bin
    (c) Notebook Deleted File Bin
    (d) Section Recycle Bin

Practice Exercises

1 Create a Notebook for a Blogger

FROM SCRATCH

Bonnie's cousin, Janetta, has been blogging on sewing topics for the past year. Janetta was excited at the possibility of using OneNote to manage her blogging activities and affiliate programs. She has asked you and Bonnie to help her create a OneNote notebook for her blogging activities. Refer to Figure 1.48 as you complete the exercise.

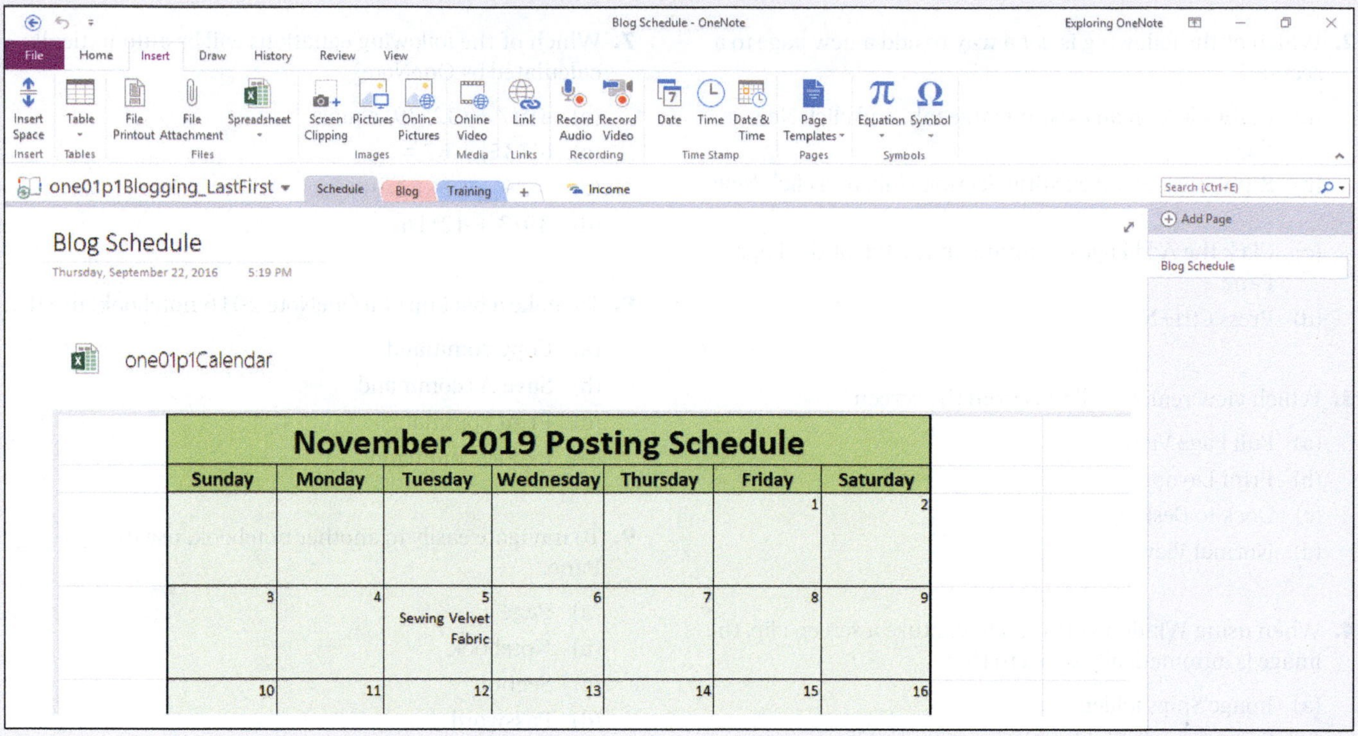

FIGURE 1.48 OneNote 2016 Blogging Notebook

DISCOVER

a. Open OneNote 2016. Click the **Navigation Pane arrow**. Click **+Add Notebook**. Ensure your OneDrive account is selected. Type **one01p1Blogging_LastFirst** as the notebook name. Click **Create Notebook**. Click **Not now**. Rename the New Section 1 section **Earnings**. Rename the Untitled page **1st QTR**. Add a page and title it **2nd QTR**.

b. Add a new section and name it **Affiliate Programs**. Name the Untitled page **Approved Programs**. Add a new page and name it **Applied Programs**.

c. Type the following on the **Approved Programs page** in the Affiliate Programs section, pressing **Enter** after each line of text, except the last line:

Amazon.com

ShareASale

Commission Junction

Pepperjam

d. Right-click in the white area to the right of the Section tabs. Click **New Section Group**. Name the section group **Income**. Drag and drop the **Earnings** and **Affiliate Programs** section tabs on the Income section group icon. Create a new section in the Income section group named **Expenses**. Rename the Untitled page as **Business Expenses**.

e. Right-click the **Earnings section tab**. Click **Delete**. Click **Yes**.

f. Click the **green return arrow** to exit the Income section group. Add a new section and name it **Blog**. Name the Untitled page **Future Articles**. Add a page and name it **Ideas for Articles**. Add a new section and name it **Schedule**. Name the Untitled page as **Blog Schedule**.

g. Click **Notebook Recycle Bin** in the History group on the History tab. Right-click the **Earnings section tab**, and click **Move or Copy**. Select the **one01p1Blogging_LastFirst** notebook, select the **Income section group**, and then click **Move**.

h. Click the **Schedule section tab** in the main notebook, and drag to move it before the **Blog** section tab. Insert *one01p1Calendar.xlsx* into the Blog Schedule page using the **Existing Excel Spreadsheet** command in the Files group of the Insert tab. Click **Insert Spreadsheet**. Click **Edit** in the top left corner of the calendar. Double-click in the cell for Tuesday, November 5. Move the pointer to the right side of the 5 in the cell. Press **Alt+Enter**. Type **Sewing Velvet Fabric**. Save the spreadsheet, and close Excel.

i. Display the Future Articles page in the Blog section, click below the date, click **Pictures** in the Images group on the Insert tab. Navigate to the student data files, select the data file named *one01p1Sewing.jpg*, and then click **Insert**. Below the photograph, type **Photo by FirstLast**, where *FirstLast* is replaced by your own name, and press **Enter**. Click **File Printout** in the Files group on the Insert tab, select *one01p1Blog1.docx*, and then click **Insert**.

j. Move the insertion point below the one01p1Blog1 data file printout text. Type ********* (this is nine asterisks) and press **Enter**. Type **I need to take photos for the blog entries attached below.** (Include the period.) Press **Enter**, click **File Attachment** in the Files group on the Insert tab, and then select *one01p1Blog2.docx*. Click **Insert**, and click **Attach File**. Use the same method to attach *one01p1Blog3.docx*.

k. Add a section titled **Training**. Rename the Untitled page **How to Blog**. Navigate to www.youtube.com in your browser, and search **how to blog**. Locate a video that explains how to blog. Copy the **URL**. Verify you are still on the How to Blog page in OneNote. Click the **Insert tab**, click **Online Video** in the Media group, paste the **URL** in the Video address box in the Insert Online Video dialog box, and then click **OK**.

l. Click the **File tab**. Click **Export**. Click **Notebook** below Export Current, select **OneNote Package (*.onepkg)** below Select Format, and then click **Export**. Navigate to your storage device in the Save As dialog box. Verify the file name is **one01p1Blogging_LastFirst**. Ensure the Save as type is **OneNote Single File Package**. Click **Save** to export your notebook to your storage device.

m. Close OneNote. Based on your instructor's directions, submit one01p1Blogging_LastFirst.

2 Add an Image, Convert an Image to Text, Add a Calculation and a Table

Janetta enjoys using her notebook. She asked for help learning to add content to the notebook. You will help her add pages, insert existing files, create a table, copy text from an image, and use OneNote to make a calculation. Refer to Figure 1.49 as you complete the exercise.

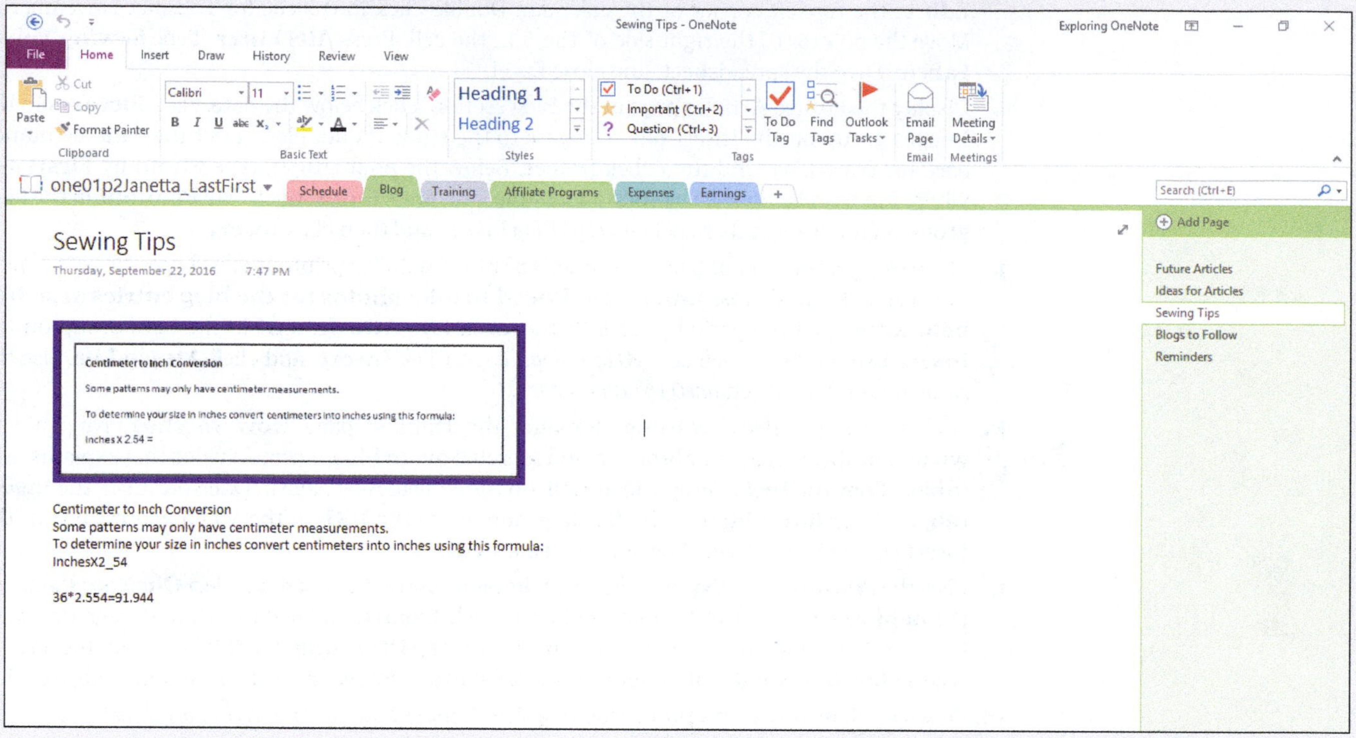

FIGURE 1.49 Add Content to OneNote 2016

a. Unpack *one01p2Janetta.onepkg* to create a new notebook titled **one01p2Janetta_LastFirst**, making sure to create it on **OneDrive**. Do not invite people to share your notebook.

b. Add a page to the **Blog section** named **Sewing Tips**, and press **Enter**. Display the Insert tab on the Ribbon, click **Pictures** in the Images group, navigate to your student data files and then select *one01p2Convert.jpg*. Click **Insert**. Right-click the image, and click **Copy Text from Picture**. Click below the image and press **Ctrl+V** to paste the text from the image.

c. Click the **Review tab** on the Ribbon. Click **Spelling** in the Spelling group. Accept any corrections recommended by the Spelling Checker. In the dialog box that states the spelling check is complete, click **OK**.

d. Click below the text copied from the picture. Type **36*2.54 =** and then press **Space**.

   The solution, 91.944, will be calculated automatically. OneNote may round the total to 91.94.

e. Add a page to the **Blog section**, name it **Blogs to Follow**. Use your browser to search for **sewing blogs**. Click on one blog from the results to open the website. Maximize the browser screen. Press **Windows+Shift+S** and click in the top left corner of the monitor screen. Hold the left mouse button and drag to the bottom right corner to select the entire screen. Expand the **one01p2Janetta_LastFirst** notebook in the Select Location in OneNote dialog box. Expand the **Blog section tab**. Click **Blogs to Follow**, and click **Send to Selected Location**.

f. Return to OneNote and add a page titled **Share** to the Earnings section. Move the page to the top of the list in the Page Pane.

g. Click the **1st QTR page tab** in the Earnings section. Click the **Insert tab**, click **Spreadsheet** in the Files group, and then click **Existing Excel Spreadsheet**. Select *one01p2Earnings*, click **Insert**, and click **Insert Spreadsheet**.

h. Click the **File tab**. Click **Print**, and click **Print Preview**. Use the following settings: **Current Page**, **Letter paper size**, **Scale content to paper width**, and **Portrait**. In the Footer, select **Page (number)**. Verify *Start page numbering at 1* is selected. Press **Windows+PrtScn**. Close Print Preview without printing. Use **Ctrl + V** to paste the screenshot on the **Share** page.

i. Click the **Applied Programs page tab** in the Affiliate Programs section. Below the page date, type the following, using Tab and Enter as needed to create the table:

Affiliate Program Application	URL	Date Applied
Juniper Online Sales	Juniperonlinesales.com	June 15, 2019
Make Sales Now	Makesalesnow.com	June 28, 2019
Infinity Online Sales	Infinityonlinesales.com	August 12, 2019

j. Click **File**. Click **Send**, and click **Send as PDF**. Type **your instructor's email address** in the To text box. In the Subject box, type **LastFirst Applied Programs**. In the message, type **My notebook is one01p2Janetta_LastFirst.**

k. Press **Windows+Shift+S**. Select the entire screen. Select the notebook, select the **Earnings section**, select the **Share page**, and then click **Send to Selected Location**. Rename the page Share page as **Send**. Do not send the email.

l. Click the **New quick note icon** in the Show hidden icons tray. Type **In my next article, ask if any of my readers would like to contribute an article or article idea to the blog.** Close the Quick Notes window. Click **Quick Notes** in the Navigation Pane. Right-click the **quick note** you just sent to Quick Notes, click **Move or Copy**, select **one01p2Janetta_LastFirst**, select the **Blog section tab**. Click **Move**. Navigate to the **Blog section tab**. Rename the Quick Notes page as **Reminders**.

> **TROUBLESHOOTING:** Page title area missing? If so, you can rename a page by right-clicking the page tab and clicking Rename. The page title area on the page will display, and you can type the page name as you normally would.

m. Click **Export** and export the entire notebook as **one01p2Janetta_LastFirst** to your storage device.

n. Close OneNote 2016. Based on your instructor's directions, submit one01p2Janetta_LastFirst.

Mid-Level Exercises

1 Create a Notebook for a Culinary Student

FROM SCRATCH

Your neighbor, Jason Belton, dreams of becoming a chef and opening his own bistro. He is attending a culinary school, and has asked you to help him set up a notebook to keep up with his classes.

a. Create a notebook using your desktop OneNote 2016 application. Name the notebook **one01m1Culinary_LastFirst**. Click **Not now**. Name the default section **Food Science**.

b. Create three additional sections titled **Pastry Techniques**, **Assignments**, and **Gastronomy**. Click the **Food Science** section, rename the Untitled page **Project**. Rename the Untitled page **Research** in the Gastronomy section.

c. Create three pages named **Notes**, **Recipes**, and **Equipment Needed** in the Pastry Techniques section. Rearrange the pages in Recipes, Notes, Equipment Needed order. Right-click the **Equipment Needed page tab**, and click **Make Subpage**.

d. Use **File Printout** on the Insert tab to insert a file printout of *one01m1Recipe1.docx* in the Recipes page.

e. Use the same method used in Step d to print the *one01m1Handout.docx* to the Pastry Techniques section Notes page.

f. Type **Supplies needed for this semester:** on the Pastry Techniques section Equipment Needed subpage. Press **Enter** twice, type **Item**, and then press **Tab** to begin creating a table. Type **Cost** and press **Enter**. Type **Deluxe cake decorating tip set**, and press **Tab**. Type **$29.99**, and press **Enter**. Type **2 pastry bags**, and press **Tab**. Type **$13.90**, and press **Enter**. Type **Pastry blender**, and press **Tab**. Type **$9.77**, and press **Enter**. Type **Cake spatula set**, and press **Tab**. Type **$35.97**.

g. Click below the table and type **$29.99 + 13.90 + 9.77 + 35.97 =** and press **Space**. The total will be $89.63.

h. Add two pages to the Pastry Techniques section titled **Cookie Recipes** and **Cake Recipes**. Move the pages below the Recipes page. Make the Cookie Recipes and Cake Recipes pages into subpages.

i. Insert the *one01m1Recipe2.jpg* picture into the Cookie Recipes subpage. Right-click the image, and copy the text from the image. Paste it to the page below the image. Make any needed corrections to the pasted text. Note that the ingredients will be in a single column.

j. Create a New Section Group named **School**. Move all sections into the *School* section group. Outside the section group, add a new section titled **Course Schedule**. Rename the Untitled page as **Class Schedule**. Insert a printout of *one01m1Courses.xlsx* below the title on the Class Schedule page.

k. Export one01m1Culinary_LastFirst to your storage device. Close OneNote. Based on your instructor's directions, submit one01m1Culinary_LastFirst.

2 Insert a Spreadsheet and an Online Video

Your sister, Sally, likes to cook, but she has trouble finding the exact recipe she wants to prepare. You created a cookbook notebook for her, but she has trouble adding new recipes. She asked you to demonstrate how to add content to the notebook.

a. Navigate to your student data files. Unpack *one01m2Food*, and save it as **one01m2Food_LastFirst**.

b. Add a new subpage to the Cookbook section titled **Pies**. Rearrange the pages in Recipes, Cakes, Candy, Cookies, Pies, and Notes order.

c. Add a subpage titled **Beef**. Move the subpage above the Cakes subpage. Add a subpage titled **Chicken**. Move the Chicken subpage above the Cookies subpage. Insert a printout of *one01m2Chicken.docx* on the Chicken subpage.

d. Navigate to **http://www.aroundmomskitchentable.com/2009/05/sweet-cool-refreshing-dessert-for.html** in your browser. Scroll to display the entire Blueberry Banana Cream Pie recipe on the screen. Press **Windows+Shift+S** and drag to select only the recipe. Expand the **one01m2Food_LastFirst** notebook, expand the **Cookbook section**, and click the **Pies subpage** in the Select Location in OneNote dialog box. Click **Send to Selected Location**.

e. Return to OneNote and add a page titled **Email**. Click the **Chicken subpage**. Prepare to send the Chicken subpage as a PDF by email to your instructor's email account. Change the Subject line to **LastFirst Chicken Recipe**. Do not click Send. Capture a **full-screen screenshot**. Navigate to the Email page. Paste the screenshot below the date. Close the Outlook window without sending or saving the email.

f. Delete the **Pies subpage tab**.

DISCOVER

g. Navigate to **YouTube.com** in your browser. Search for **basic cooking terms**. Select a video, and copy the **URL**. Navigate to the **Notes page**, click below the date, and then press **Ctrl+V**.

h. Click **Notebook Recycle Bin** in the History group on the History tab. Right-click on the **Pies subpage tab**, and click **Move or Copy**. Select the **one01m2Food_LastFirst** notebook, select the **Cookbook section**, and then click **Move**. Navigate to the Cookbook section tab. Move the **Pies page tab** above the Notes page tab. Make the **Pies page** a subpage.

i. Navigate to the **Pies subpage**. Insert a printout of *one01m2Pie.docx* below the Blueberry Banana Cream Pie recipe.

j. Export the Notebook to your storage media, using the name **one01m2Food_LastFirst**.

k. Close OneNote. Based on your instructor's directions, submit one01m2Food_LastFirst.

Beyond the Classroom

Job Search

**General
Case**

In preparation for graduation, use the Internet to research at least five companies for whom you are interested in working, based on your field of study. Use the skills you learned in this chapter to create a job search OneNote notebook and name it **one01b1JobSearch_LastFirst**. For each company you research, create a section. In each section, include pages for company history and facts, information concerning the procedure for applying, and the types of positions available. The notebook should also have at least two subpages. Select at least one position and use the Internet to research salary ranges for that position in your area. Record your findings on a page in the notebook. Group the sections in a section group named **Job Search**. Based on your instructor's directions, submit one01b1JobSearch_LastFirst.

Recover Deleted Sections

**DISASTER
RECOVERY**

While working with the blogging notebook you and Bonnie created for her, Janetta accidentally deleted the Income section group tab. Janetta called you for help in retrieving the deleted section group. Create a new Word document and save it as **one01b2Recover_LastFirst**. Type your name and the current date on the first two lines at the top of the page. Using a numbered list, write step-by-step instructions explaining how to find the deleted section group in the Notebook Recycle Bin and retrieve it. Save the document. Based on your instructor's directions, submit one01b2Recover_LastFirst.

Capstone Exercise

Programming Team Notebook

Search It, Inc. is an ambitious search engine company for corporate clients. As an administrative assistant for Search It, Inc., you have been asked to create a OneNote notebook for the Server Side Programming Team. The notebook will contain section groups, sections, and pages to provide information and announcements to the team.

Create a Notebook with Sections and Pages

You will create a notebook that contains section groups, sections, pages, and subpages to provide information and announcements to the team.

a. Create a notebook named **one01c1Capstone_LastFirst** and save it to your storage device. Do not share the notebook.

b. Create four sections titled **Activities**, **Notes**, **Contacts**, and **Announcements**.

c. Rename the Untitled pages in the sections you created as follows:

Section Name	Page Name
Activities	**Company Activities**
Notes	**HTML Notes**
Contacts	**Team Contacts**
Announcements	**Team Announcement**

d. Add two subpages below the Team Announcements page titled **Company Stationery** and **Team Shirts**.

Add and Edit Existing Content

You will attach files, type text into pages, paste text into a page, and then edit the information you copied and pasted into the notebook. One of your team members recently married, so you will correct her last name in the contacts list.

a. Attach the *one01c1Evaluation.docx* file to the Announcements section **Team Announcements page**, and press **Enter**. Insert a file printout of *one01c1Announcements.docx*.

b. Navigate to the Announcements section **Company Stationery subpage**. Type **As of August 1, 2019, all written correspondence to vendors and suppliers must be typed on company letterhead stationery. The letterhead template is attached below.** Press **Enter** twice. Attach *one01c1Letterhead.dotx*.

c. Insert a file printout of *one01c1Picnic.docx* in the Activities section **Company Activities page**.

d. Open *one01c1Addresses.docx* in Word 2016. Select and copy all contents. Display the **Contacts section** in OneNote. Paste the team addresses on the Contacts section Team Contacts page. Add a **blank line** above Carla Gardner's name. Type the following on the blank line, pressing **Enter** after each line:

Your name
1111 W. Somewhere Dr.
Liberty Mountain, TX 78642
(555) 555-1234

FirstInitialLastName@searchit.com

e. Change Carla Gardner's last name to **Powell**.

Delete a Section, Retrieve a Deleted Section, and Rearrange Section Tabs

Your manager requested the section tabs be rearranged into alphabetical order. You accidentally delete the Announcements section tab while working with the notebook. You will retrieve the section.

a. Delete the **Announcements section tab**.

b. Click **Notebook Recycle Bin** in the History section on the History tab. Move the **Announcements section tab** back to the one01c1Capstone_LastFirst notebook.

c. Rearrange the section tabs until they are in this order:

Activities, **Announcements**, **Contacts**, **Notes**.

Create a Screen Clip, Add a Link, and Copy Text from a Picture

The Server Side Team leader needs information on HTML on the Notes section HTML Notes page. You will create a screen clip (screenshot) and insert it into the notebook to show him how to convert text in an image into editable text.

a. Navigate to **http://www.w3schools.com/html/** in your browser. Click **HTML Introduction** in the left menu bar. Scroll down the page until you can see *A Simple HTML Document*. Use **Windows+Shift+S** and drag to capture a screenshot of the code in the HTML Example box, starting with *A Simple HTML Document* and ending with *</html>*. Send the screenshot to the Notes section **HTML Notes page**.

b. Click below the screenshot. Use the Link command in the Insert tab to insert a link to the URL in the previous step, with the link text as **W3 Schools Computer Training**.

c. Copy the text from the screenshot image you added to the HTML Notes page, and paste the text below the link. Make corrections to the pasted text, so that the text matches that in the image.

Add a Picture, a Table, and a Calculation

Your team is selling team shirts. You will insert your team logo on a subpage, add text, and then create a table of prices. Below the table you will provide instructions on figuring total due on shirt orders.

a. Navigate to the Announcements section Team Shirts subpage. Type **Team Shirt with Logo** and bold the text. Press **Enter** twice. Insert the **one01c1Logo.png** picture file. Press **Enter** twice. Type **Carla and Abe have finished the team logo for our team shirts**. Press **Enter** twice.

b. Type the following, pressing **Tab** after the first two column entries and **Enter** after the third column entry:

Shirt Color	Sizes	Price
White	S, M, L, XL	$15.99
White	XXL, XXXL	$18.99
Black	S, M, L, XL	$15.99
Black	XXL, XXXL	$18.99

c. Below the table, type **Be sure to add 8.5% tax to your order. To figure the total due on your order, multiply the shirt subtotal by 1.085**. Press **Enter**.

d. Type **Example: (2*$18.99)*1.085 =** and then press the **Space**.

OneNote rounds the total to $41.21.

Use the New Quick Note Tool

You will search for and copy information in your browser and use the New quick note tool to send the note to your OneNote notebook.

a. Search for **HTML add video** in your browser search engine and find a website that explains how to add

video to an HTML document. Copy the article title and the first two paragraphs of the information. Click the **New quick note tool** in the Show hidden icons tray. Paste the **copied text** into the Quick Notes window. Close the Quick Notes window and the browser.

b. Navigate to **Quick Notes** in the Navigation pane in OneNote. Move the page you just created in Quick Notes to the Notes section of your one01c1Capstone_LastFirst notebook. In OneNote, rename the page as **HTML Adding Video**.

Check Spelling, Create Section Groups with Sections, Copy Sections, and Export the Notebook

You will check the spelling in each section. Your manager has not yet decided whether to keep all teams in the same notebook, or create new notebooks for each team, so you will create section groups for other teams and add sections to the section groups. After you complete your manager's requirements for the notebook, export it to create a backup.

a. Check spelling on all sections, making any necessary corrections.

b. Create two section groups named **CSP Team** and **Mainframe Team**.

c. Create four sections titled **Activities**, **Notes**, **Contacts**, and **Announcements** in the CSP Team section group. Copy each section in the CSP Team section group into the Mainframe Team section group. Verify section tabs are in Activities, Announcements, Contacts, and Notes order in both section groups. The teams will each add additional information to their sections.

d. Export one01c1Capstone_LastFirst to your storage device.

e. Close OneNote. Based on your instructor's directions, submit one01c1Capstone_LastFirst.

OneNote 2016

Formatting and Collaborating Online with OneNote

LEARNING OUTCOME

- You will demonstrate an understanding of how to use OneNote tools and templates and how to use OneNote to collaborate with others.

OBJECTIVES & SKILLS: After you read this chapter, you will be able to:

CASE STUDY | Student Intern

Bonnie Duckett's new OneNote 2016 skills have landed her a student intern position with Search It, an online search-engine company. As an undergraduate student majoring in Information Systems Management in the College of Technology & Computing at Pearson University, Bonnie uses OneNote to help track her courses. She develops OneNote notebooks for others, too. In her internship, she creates OneNote notebooks for her team and for her manager.

CHAPTER 2

Tools, Templates, and Collaboration with OneNote 2016, OneNote Online, and OneNote App

FIGURE 2.1 College Notebook

OneNote 2016, Windows 10, Microsoft Corporation

CASE STUDY | Student Intern

Starting Files	Files to be Submitted
one02h1Spring.xlsx	one02h1Tools_LastFirst.onepkg
one02h2Addresses.docx	one02h2Apps_LastFirst.onepkg
one02h2List.docx	
one02h2Preambles.docx	
one02h2Topics.pdf	

Use Tools and Templates

OneNote 2016 provides many tools to help you organize and format your notes and pages. If all the text in your notebook was the same font, size, color, and weight, it would make the text hard to read. Just as this book uses headings and subheadings to break up the text into discrete sections, using formatting will give organization to your notebook and save you time and frustration when searching a page for specific information.

In this section, you will learn about formatting text, applying a template, and using pen and drawing tools. In addition, you will learn how to check the spelling in your notes, use the built-in thesaurus to find just the right word, add tags to notes, and password protect a section.

Using Tools and Templates

STEP 1 ▶▶ Formatting text using color, size, weight, and style can add interest and emphasis. For instance, using bold, red text to indicate information that may be on a final exam would help it be more memorable and easier to locate on the page. Too much formatting can be a hindrance, however. If all text is red and bold, finding specific information to study for an exam will be difficult. Some colors, such as yellow or cyan, are difficult to read, especially if there are long paragraphs of the text formatted with these colors.

When formatting text, keep in mind the reason you are formatting it. Use bold, italics, and color in a consistent manner. Basic black text on a white screen is the most easily read combination, but using some color can be helpful in locating specific information in your notes or in memorizing content.

Formatting is applied to text in the same way as in other Office applications, using the Basic Text group on the Home tab (see Figure 2.2). You can also copy text formatting from one item to another using the **Format Painter** in the Clipboard group of the Home tab. Click Format Painter, and drag the Format Painter pointer over the text you need to change. After you release the left mouse button, the Format Painter automatically turns off. If you are making multiple changes—for instance, changing all the page titles in all pages of all sections—you can format the title on one page, select the text, double-click Format Painter, and then navigate to each page and drag the pointer over the title to make the format changes. After you complete making the formatting changes, click Format Painter again to turn it off. A single click enables you to copy the format to another area once, whereas double-clicking the Format Painter toggles it on, and it will remain on until you click the button again.

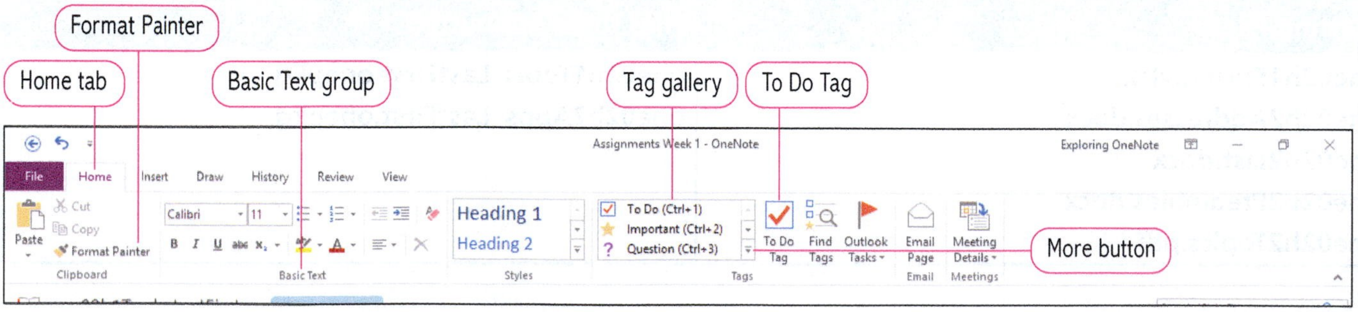

FIGURE 2.2 The OneNote Home Tab

Apply a Page Template

In OneNote, **page templates** are used to add predesigned page designs and formats to new pages in your notebook. Using page templates saves time in creating pages and adds consistency to the overall notebook design. Page templates are available in the Pages group on the Insert tab. Click Page Templates to open the **Templates pane**, which provides access to predesigned templates installed with OneNote, including Academic, Blank, Business, Decorative, and Planners templates (see Figure 2.3). When you insert a template, a new page will be created.

To use a template, complete the following steps:

1. Select the appropriate section.
2. Click the Page Templates arrow in the Pages group on the Insert tab, and click Page templates.
3. Click the major heading desired in the Templates pane, such as Academic.
4. Click on the specific template. Some templates will have background colors and images, whereas others will be simple or blank.

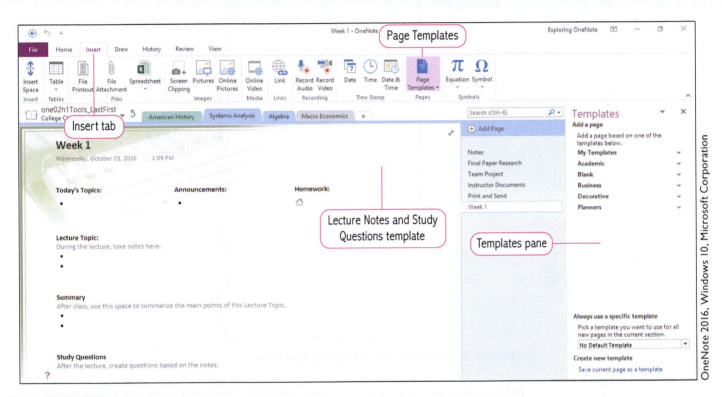

FIGURE 2.3 The Templates Pane

For a notebook that contains sections for each class, you might add a Simple Lecture Notes page template from the Academic templates to each course section. This page template provides a preformatted page with places for homework and notes.

Page colors can also be changed using a template in the Blank heading. If page colors are changed, you may also want to change the section tab to match the color. To change the color of a section tab, right-click on the tab, point to Section Color, and then select the desired color from the list. There is no way to add a template to a page that has already been created. However, you can create a template page, copy the contents of an existing page, and then paste the contents into a template page. You will have two copies of the same page—one with the template and one without. Delete the original page if you do not want duplicates of the page content in your notebook.

Create a Page Template

If you need a template that is not available in the Templates pane, you can create your own template. To create a template, format a page as needed, click the *Save current page as a template* command at the bottom of the Templates pane, name the template, and then click Save. OneNote will create a new template heading titled My Templates in the Templates pane (see Figure 2.4). To use your page template, use the same method as applying any other page template.

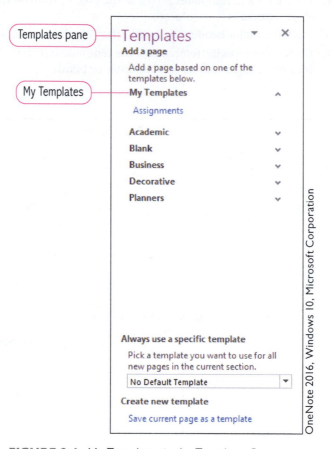

FIGURE 2.4 My Templates in the Templates Pane

TIP: MAKE IMAGES PART OF THE PAGE BACKGROUND
To add an image as a background item, insert the image on a notebook page, right-click on the image, and then click Set Picture as Background. This is only reversible by using the Undo button, so verify that the image is in the correct location before making other changes.

Create a Wiki

A **wiki** is a shared electronic database or file with content that can be changed, added to, or deleted by anyone with whom the wiki has been shared. For instance, when an instructor assigns a group project, a notebook can be created and shared with all team members, giving them all permission to update and delete the notebook contents to create a team wiki. Adding links to other pages in the notebook might make the notebook more useful to the team (see Figure 2.5).

To add links to other pages in a OneNote notebook to create a wiki, complete the following steps:

1. Type two left brackets (**[[**) in any line of text.
2. Type the page title of an existing page in the notebook.
3. Type two right brackets (**]]**) after the page title. OneNote will create a link to that page.

If you want to add a page that does not exist, type the title for the new page. OneNote will create the new page, with a link pointing to it. Until you add notes to the new page, the link underline will be a dotted line.

Use Links to Add a Table of Contents to a Notebook

STEP 2 ⟫ In time, a notebook may become large enough to be unwieldy, making it difficult to find the specific information you need. A table of contents (TOC) that lists links to all the sections in the notebook makes it much more convenient to locate a particular section. If a section contains many pages, a TOC page will help you locate specific pages. There are two ways to create a TOC for your notebook.

To create a table of contents, complete the following set of steps:

1. Create a new Table of Contents section or page.
2. Right-click any section tab or page tab. If you are linking to a section, click Copy Link to Section. If you are linking to a page, click Copy Link to Page.
3. Click below the page title on the Table of Contents page, and press Ctrl+V to paste the link to the section or page. OneNote will automatically add the section or page title to the page. Press Enter. Repeat steps 2–3 to add each section or page tab to the TOC.

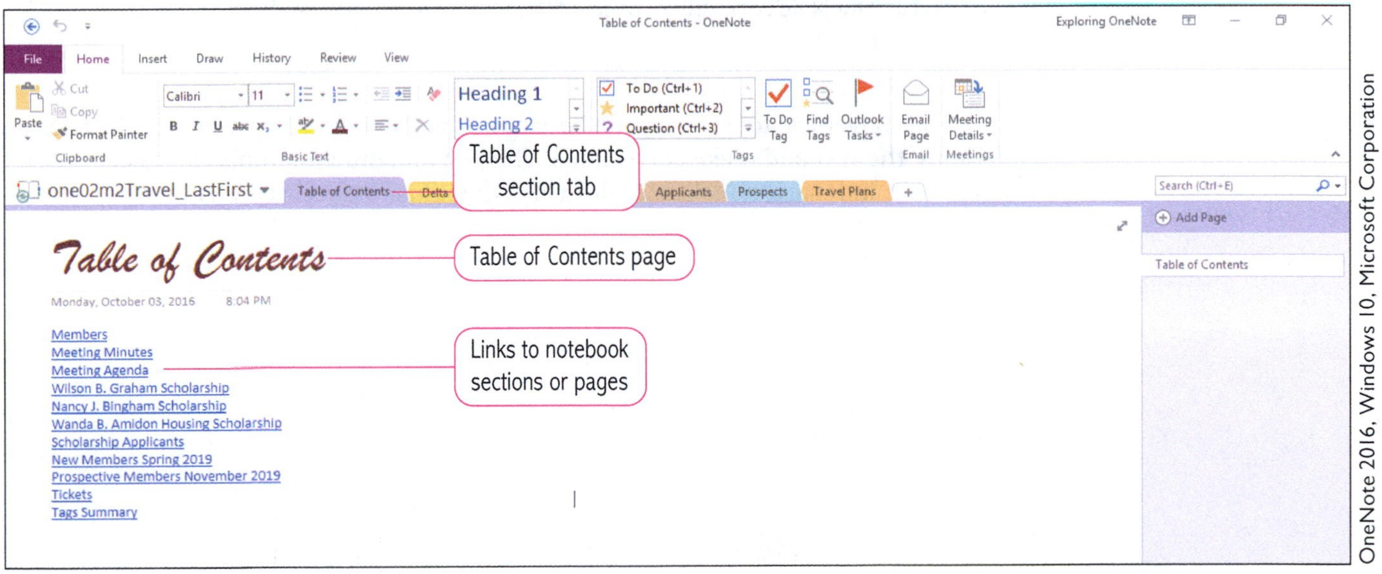

FIGURE 2.5 Create a Table of Contents

While creating a TOC using the above method avoids typing the section or page names, there may be occasions when a section or page name may need to be entered manually. In those instances, a different method can be used.

To manually add a section or page title to a TOC, complete the following steps:

1. Type a list of all the section tab names or page tab names.
2. Highlight the section tab or page tab name you typed.
3. Click Link in the Links group on the Insert tab.
4. Click the + sign at the left of the notebook name in the Link dialog box.
5. Click the section group name if the section is in a group, then click the name of the section or page to which you are linking. Click OK.

Convert Handwritten Notes Created with Pen and Drawing Tools to Typed Text

In OneNote, the pen and drawing tools are primarily designed for use with a tablet and either your finger or a stylus. Whereas it is possible to use these features with a mouse, the results may not be suitable for notetaking. Notes written into the page area can be changed to typed text using the Ink to Text command, as shown in Figure 2.6.

One of the most useful features of OneNote is the ability to take notes directly on the page using a touch device and the OneNote app. On a touch device, using the Draw tab commands you can take handwritten notes in class, sync the notes to OneNote 2016, and convert the notes to typed text when you get to your desktop.

To change handwritten notes to text, complete the following steps:

1. Open the page with handwritten notes.
2. Click Lasso Select in the Tools group on the Draw tab.
3. Use the pointer to draw a shape around the text to be converted.
4. Right-click the selected text, and click Ink to Text.
5. Verify OneNote correctly converted the text. If necessary, make corrections.

The conversion to text may not be exact, so you may have to click into the container holding the text and make corrections. The pen and drawing tools can also be used for creating mind maps, sketches, or drawings that illustrate your typed notes.

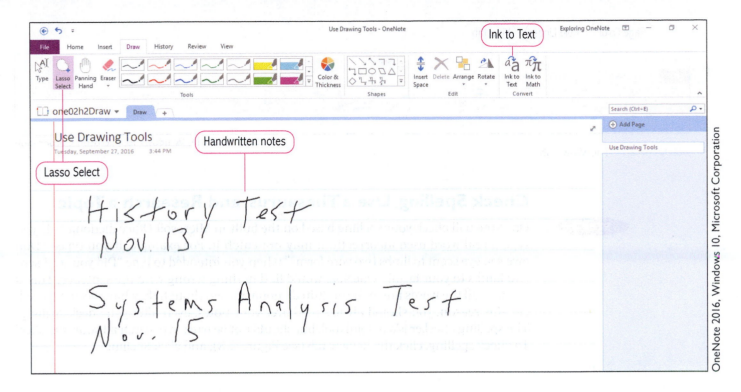

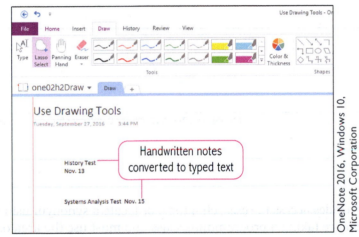

FIGURE 2.6 Notes Written with a Stylus Converted to Text

Add Rule Lines

One of the greatest difficulties in writing with a finger or stylus on a tablet screen is keeping the text lines straight. Adding rule lines makes writing on a tablet screen similar to using a regular spiral notebook. You can find a variety of ruled line options in the Rule Lines command in the Page Setup group on the View tab (see Figure 2.7).

You also have the option of using the Always Create Pages with Rule Lines command to ensure you will have rule lines every time you add a page. Rule line color can be changed by clicking the Rule Lines arrow. Select Rule Line Color in the menu list, and select a rule line color. In addition to adding rule lines, you can also add color to a notebook page. On the View tab, in the Page Setup group, click the Page Color arrow and select a color.

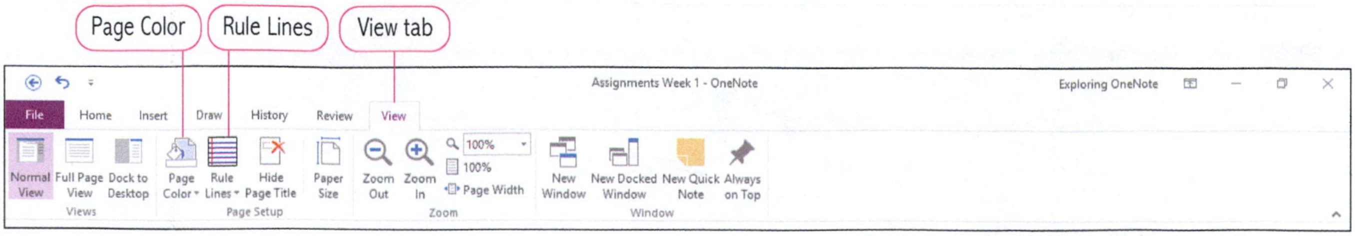

Page Color   Rule Lines   View tab

FIGURE 2.7   The View Tab

OneNote 2016, Windows 10, Microsoft Corporation

Check Spelling, Use a Thesaurus, and Research a Topic

STEP 3 ▶▶ OneNote will check your spelling based on the built-in Microsoft Office dictionary. If you type a real word used incorrectly, it may not catch it. For example, if you typed "Dud ewe sea eye scent to limbs two yore form?" when you intended to type "Did you see I sent two lambs to your farm?" OneNote would find nothing wrong with the sentence. This is because all the words are in the built-in dictionary, even though they have been misused. For this reason, you should always read over your notes, even after you check spelling. The spelling checker is a helpful tool, but should not be trusted to catch all your mistakes. To check spelling, click the Review tab (see Figure 2.8), and click Spelling.

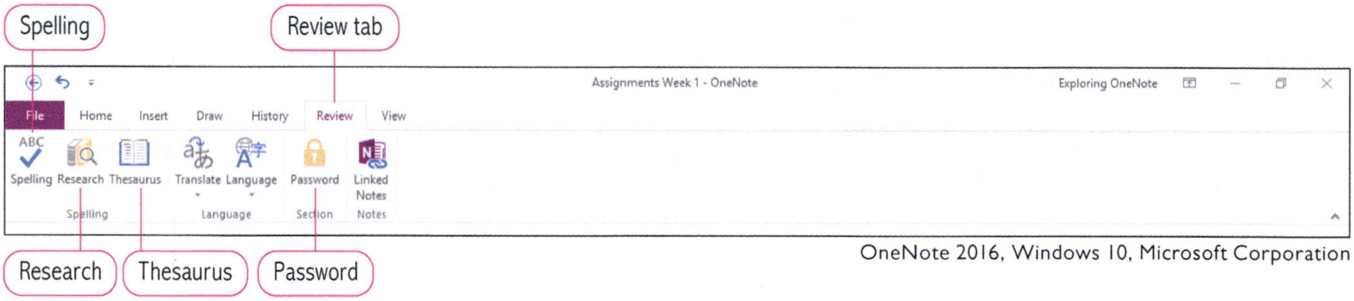

Spelling   Review tab

Research   Thesaurus   Password

FIGURE 2.8   The Review Tab

OneNote 2016, Windows 10, Microsoft Corporation

The Review tab also provides access to research a topic or locate a synonym using the thesaurus. Suppose you are taking a programming class and must use the area of a circle in a program that will solve math problems when you input variables, but you do not remember the formula to find the area of a circle. Click Research in the Spelling group on the Review tab. In the Research pane, type in *area of a circle*. OneNote uses Bing to search the Internet and returns results that may be what you need. Click on the link below the search results you are interested in reviewing, and your default Web browser will open to display the website.

You can easily use the Windows+Shift+S key combination to take a screen clipping that gives the basic information about the area of a circle and provides the formula. To do this, with your browser open to the information you need, drag to select the portion of the screen you want. In the Select Location in OneNote dialog box, select the section or page on which to insert the clipping, and click Send to Selected Location. The clipping is sent to the OneNote location you selected.

> **TIP: BROWSER WEB CLIPPING**
> A new function of the Microsoft Edge browser is the ability to take a Web clipping directly from the page and incorporate it into OneNote. To take a Web clipping in the Edge browser, click the Make a Web Note button, click the Clip button, select the area to clip, and then paste the clipping into your OneNote page.

Apply a Password

STEP 4 In OneNote, you can password protect individual sections of a notebook. This feature should be used with care. If you forget the password, you cannot retrieve the password, and will never be able to access your information. If you are using OneNote on your own computer and will not have others using your computer, password protection may not be necessary. However, if you share your notebook with someone else, **password protection** prevents others from accessing sensitive information. Password protection can be added to a section in your desktop application using the Password Protection dialog box (see Figure 2.9), but at the time of this writing, this option was not available in OneNote Online.

To apply password protection to a section, complete the following steps:

1. Ensure the section you want to password protect is the current active section.
2. Click Password in the Section group on the Review tab.
3. Click Set Password in the Password Protection pane.
4. Type your password in the Enter Password text box in the Password Protection dialog box.
5. Retype the password in the Confirm Password text box.
6. Click OK.

If the passwords match, OneNote will password protect your section. If not, OneNote will display a message box with the message *The password confirmation does not match.* You will be required to re-enter the password and confirmation password. Again, if you lose or forget the password, you will not be able to recover your notes. For security, do not put the password on a sticky note and stick it to your monitor or under your keyboard. It sounds silly, but many people do just that. If you must write it down to remember it, put the paper with the password in a safe place.

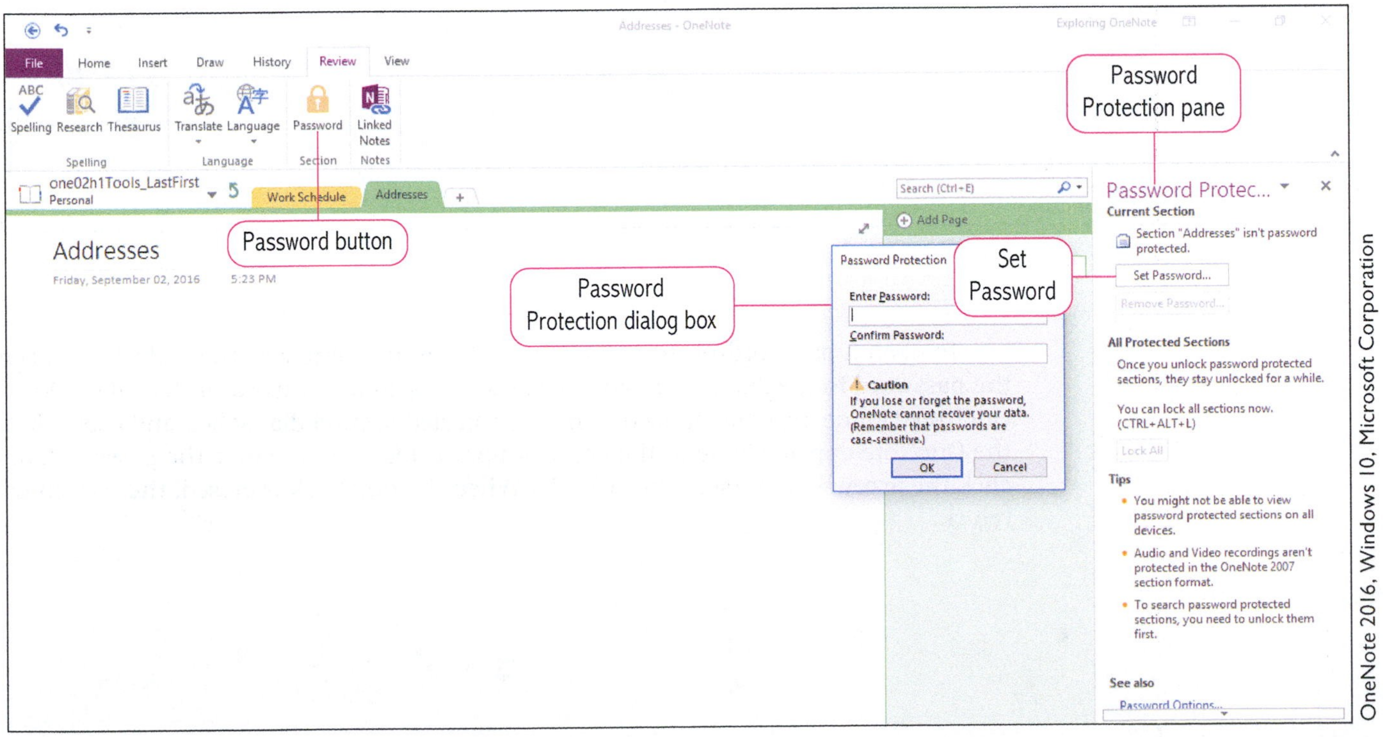

FIGURE 2.9 Password Protection Dialog Box

While you cannot password protect an entire notebook, all the sections can be password protected in a notebook using the same or a different password for each. Once the password is set, you must provide the password to access the section. When password-protected sections are unlocked, they stay unlocked until OneNote is closed. The section will be locked when the notebook is reopened. To relock the section or sections without closing OneNote, you can use the Lock All button in the Password Protection pane, or alternatively, you can use the Ctrl+Alt+L key combination.

In the Password Protection pane, you can change the password or remove the password, but you will need to know the current password to make those changes. To remove a password, click in the center of the password-protected section and type the password in the Protected Section dialog box. In the Password Protection pane, click Remove Password. In the Remove Password dialog box, type the password, and click OK.

To change the password, click Change Password in the Password Protection pane (see Figure 2.10). In the Change Password dialog box, enter the current password in the Old Password text box, type the new password in the Enter New Password text box, and then retype the new password in the Confirm Password text box. Click OK.

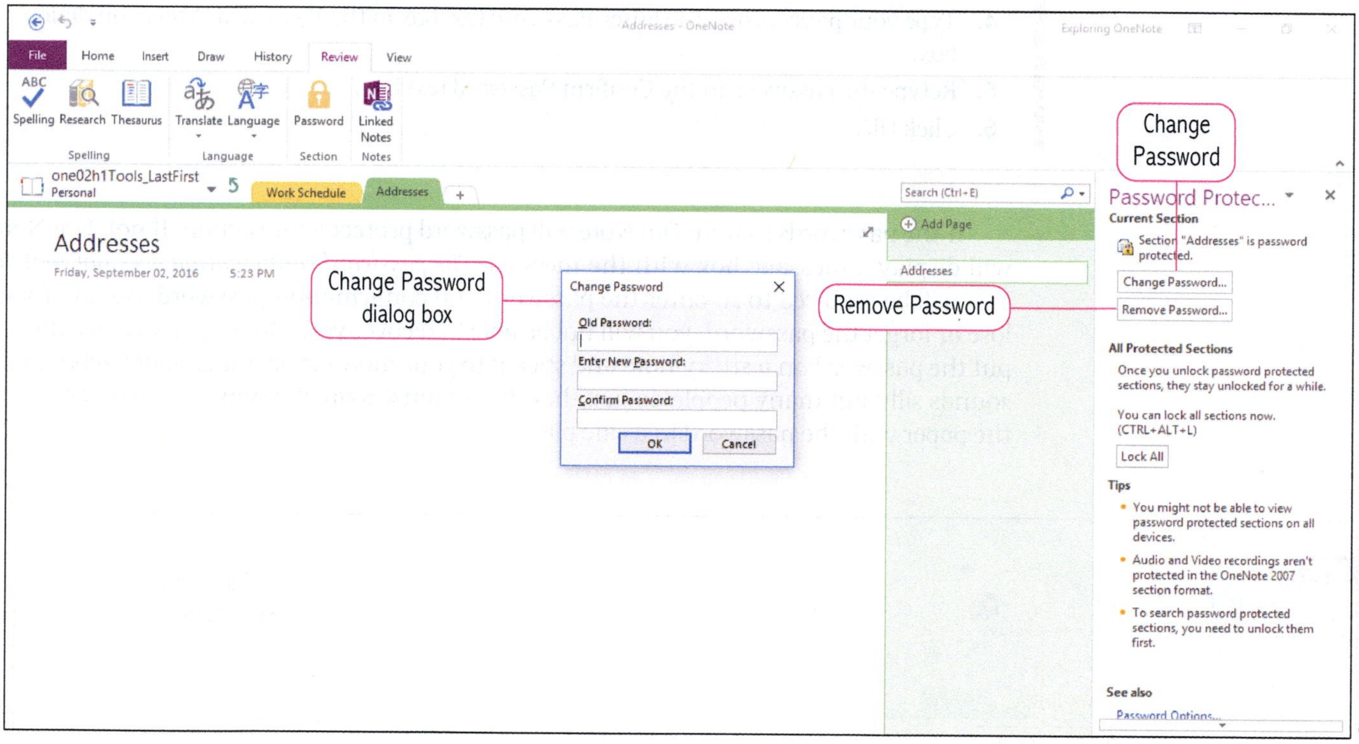

OneNote 2016, Windows 10, Microsoft Corporation

FIGURE 2.10 Change a Password

To open a password-protected section, click in the center of the locked page, type the password in the dialog box, and click OK. To open a password-protected section in OneNote Online, type the password in the Protected Section dialog box and click OK. In the OneNote app, navigate to the password-protected section, enter the password, and click the arrow button (see Figure 2.11). When the notebook is closed, the section will relock.

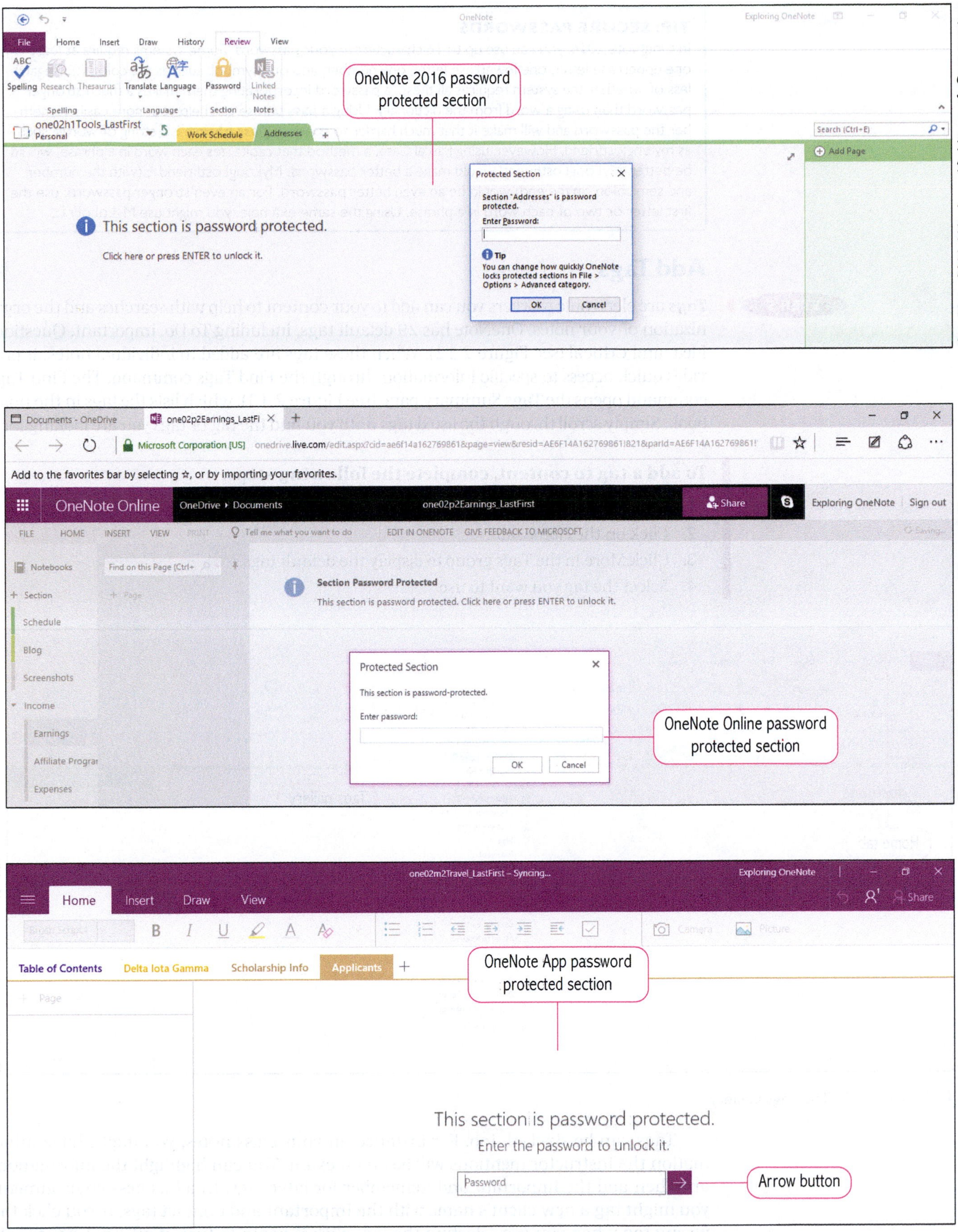

FIGURE 2.11 Open a Password Protected Section in OneNote 2016, OneNote Online, and OneNote App

TIP: SECURE PASSWORDS

In OneNote 2016, you can use up to 16 characters in your password. Some systems require at least one uppercase letter, one lowercase letter, one number, and one symbol, such as the colon (:). Regardless of whether the system requires all these, a password incorporating them makes a much stronger password than using a word from the dictionary. Using a pass phrase can help you more easily remember the password and will make it that much harder to guess. A ***pass phrase*** is a string of words, such as mylonglostfriend. However, using Pascal Case, a method that capitalizes each word in a phrase, would be better. MyLongLostFriend would make a better password. MyLongLostFriend1; (with the number and semicolon on the end) would be an even better password. For an even stronger password, use the first letter or two of each word in a phrase. Using the same example, you might use MyLoLoFr1;.

Add Tags

STEP 5 ***Tags*** are electronic markers you can add to your content to help with searches and the organization of your notes. OneNote has 29 default tags, including To Do, Important, Question, Idea, and Critical (see Figure 2.12). When these tags are added to individual notes, it provides quick access to specific information through the Find Tags command. The Find Tags command opens the Tags Summary pane (see Figure 2.13), which lists the tags in the notebook. Simply scroll through the listed tags until you find the tag or tags you are looking for.

To add a tag to content, complete the following steps:

1. Highlight the note or content you want to tag.
2. Click on the Home tab.
3. Click More in the Tags group to display the default tags.
4. Select the tag you want to use.

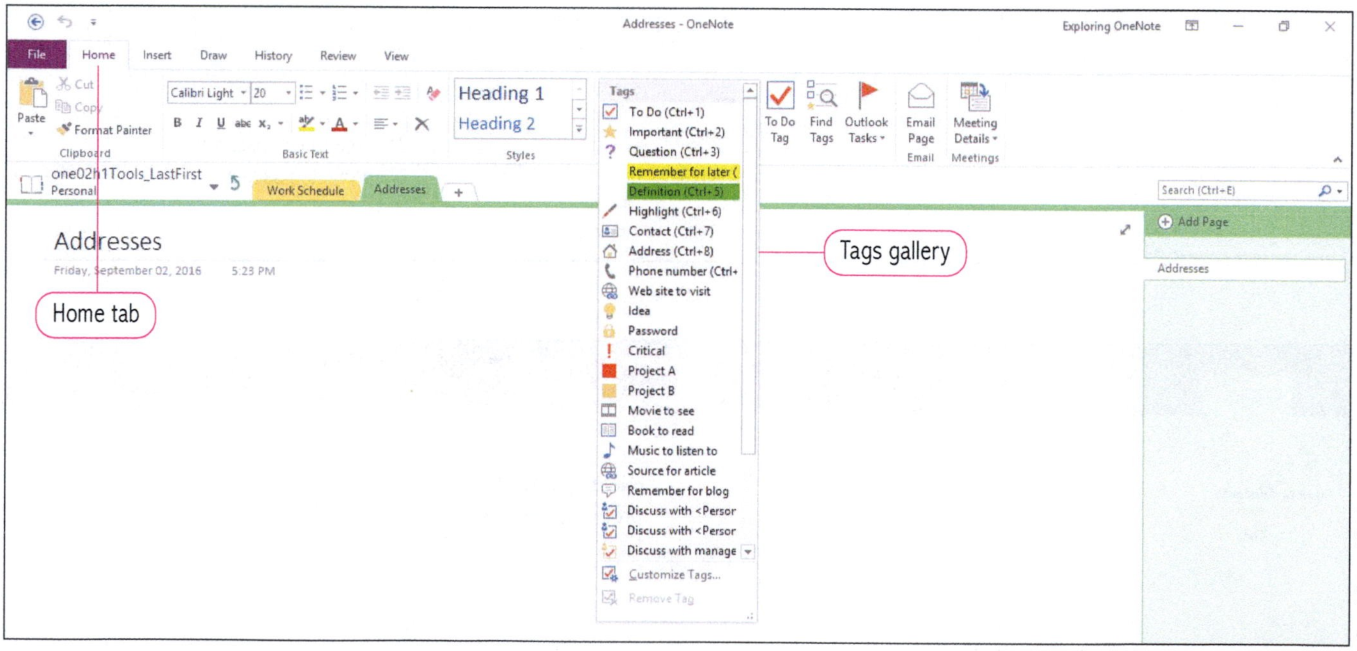

OneNote 2016, Windows 10, Microsoft Corporation

FIGURE 2.12 The Tags Gallery

Tags can be stacked, too. For instance, in your class notes, you might have information the instructor mentions will be on an exam. You can highlight the information, and then add the Important and Remember for later tags. In a business environment, you might tag a new client's name with the Important and Contact tags. If you click the wrong tag when you are selecting the tag, click it again to turn it off. Tags are ***toggle commands***, meaning they are either on or off. Click a tag once and it turns on and displays the icon or highlighting selected. Click the same tag again, and it turns off, removing the tag from your note.

Search Notes

Searching for specific content in a notebook could be frustrating if the notebook has several months or even years of notes in it. The search bar enables you to key a **search term**, a phrase or keyword relevant to the content you are trying to find, and select which notebook or section to search for the specified information. To search for specific notes or key terms use the search box as instructed in Chapter 1.

A results pane appears listing all locations of the search term in the selected search scope.

Find Tags

Another way to search for and find specific content in a notebook is to use the **Find Tags** command. Located in the Tags group on the Home tab, the Find Tags command gives you the option to search a page, section, notebook, or all notebooks on your storage device.

To use the Find Tags command, complete the following steps:

1. Click Find Tags in the Tags group on the Home tab.
2. Select a grouping category in the Tags Summary pane (see Figure 2.13).
3. Select the page, section, notebook, or other area to search in the Search criteria box.
4. Click the desired tag link to navigate to the tag location in the notebook.

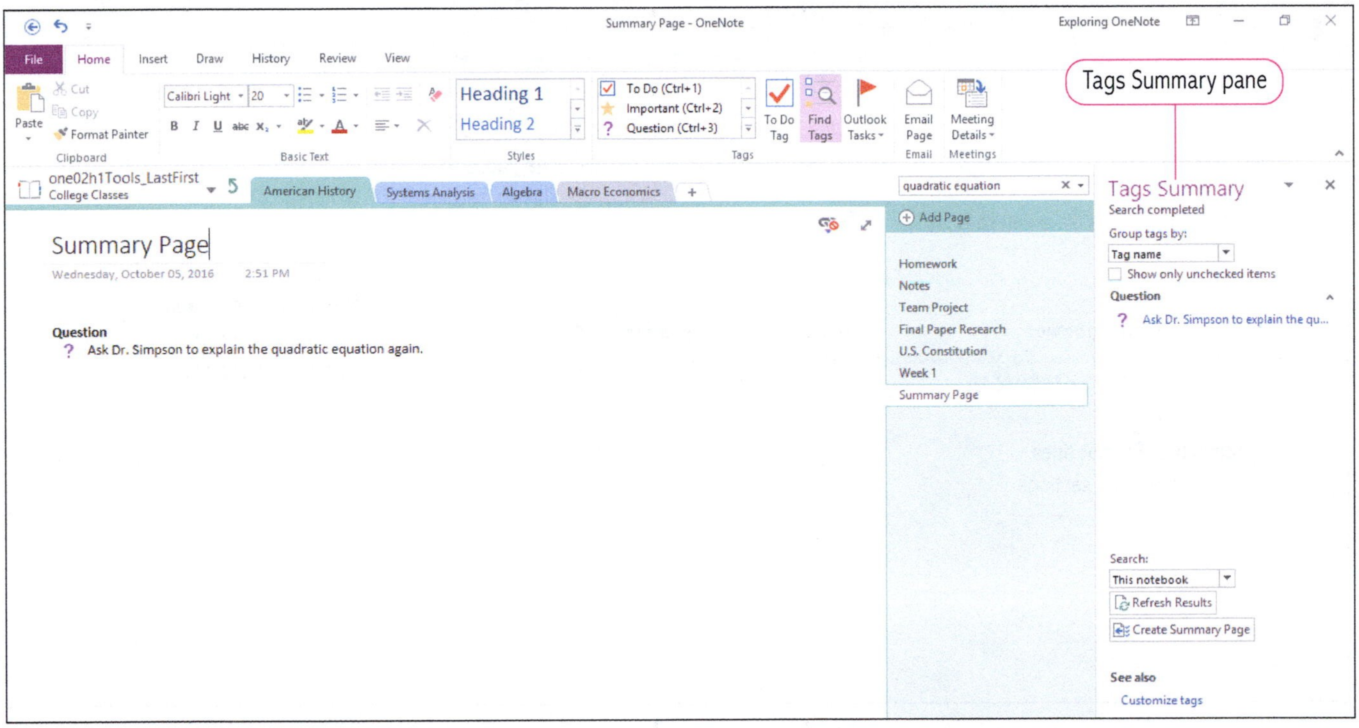

FIGURE 2.13 Tags Summary Pane

Quick Concepts ✓

1. What is the advantage of using a page template instead of creating your own page design? **p. 64**

2. Give three examples of when you would use the commands on the Review tab. **p. 70**

3. Why is using a pass phrase a good idea? Give an example of a pass phrase that would be difficult to guess. **p. 71**

4. Explain three instances when you would add tags to your notebook content. **p. 74**

Hands-On Exercises

Skills covered: Use Formatting Tools • Insert a Page Template • Create a Page Template • Use Format Painter • Use Links to Add a Table of Contents • Check Spelling • Research a Topic • Apply a Password • Add Tags • Find Tags

1 Use Tools and Templates

After reviewing her notebook, Bonnie has decided it needs some color and design to make the information more memorable. You will help her learn to add formatting to her text, apply a page template to make her notes pages more useful, create a page template, check spelling, and use a thesaurus to find the correct word. You will also help her learn to research a topic from within OneNote, apply a password, search her notes, and add tags to her notes.

STEP 1 ▶▶ **FORMAT TEXT, APPLY A PAGE TEMPLATE, AND CREATE A TEMPLATE**

In this section, you will format text previously added to the notebook in Chapter 1, Hands-On Exercises 1 and 2. To enhance the visual design and usefulness of pages, you will apply a different page template to several pages, and create a new template for use in the Assignments section. Refer to Figure 2.14 as you complete Step 1.

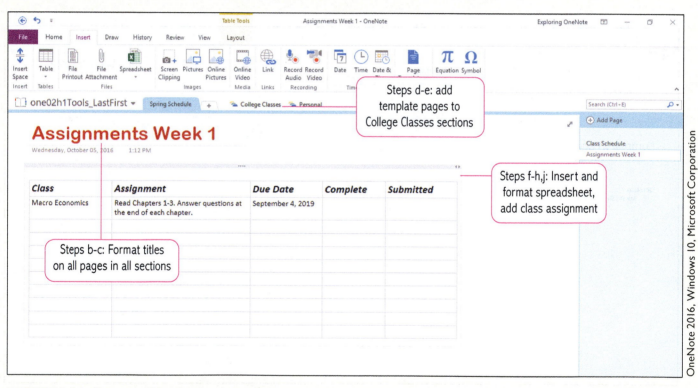

FIGURE 2.14 Formatted Notebook

a. Use Windows File Explorer, locate and double-click *one02h1Tools.onepkg* to unpack the notebook. Save it as **one02h1Tools_LastFirst**.

b. Click on the **Notes** page in the Systems Analysis section in the College Classes section group, and highlight the Notes page title. Click the **Font arrow** in the Basic Text group on the Home tab. Change the font to **Arial Rounded MT Bold**. Change the font color to **Red, Darker 25%**, and the font size to **28**. With the title selected, double-click **Format Painter** in the Clipboard group to toggle the Format Painter on. Click each **page** in the

Systems Analysis section and drag the **Format Painter pointer** to select and format the title to the new format. Click Format Painter in the Clipboard group once to toggle off the Format Painter when all changes are done.

c. Click the **American History section tab**. Use the Format Painter to format the page titles for all pages in the section using the same formatting as used on the Systems Analysis page titles. Change the format of all page titles in the Algebra and Macro Economics sections. Click **Format Painter** once to toggle it off.

d. Click the **Systems Analysis section tab**. Click the **Page Templates arrow** in the Pages group on the Insert tab, and click **Page Templates** at the bottom of the list. Click **Academic** in the Templates pane, and click **Lecture Notes and Study Questions**. Title the new page **Week 1**. Add the **History Class Notes** template page to the American History section, and the **Math/Science Class Notes** template page to the Algebra section, and title them both **Week 1**. Close the Templates pane.

e. Rename the Fall Schedule section tab as **Spring Schedule**. Select the file name and the spreadsheet on the page and press **Delete**. Insert the Existing Excel Spreadsheet file named *one02h1Spring.xlsx*. Add a page and rename the Untitled page as **Assignments Week 1**. Select the **page title** on the Assignments Week 1 page. Change the font to **Arial Rounded MT Bold**. Change the font color to **Red, Darker 25%**, and the font size to **28**. Click below the date and press **Enter**.

> **TROUBLESHOOTING:** Can't find the Fall Schedule section tab? Click the Navigate to parent section group arrow (green arrow to right Notebook Pane tab) to return to the main notebook.

f. Type the following, pressing **Tab** after each, and then pressing **Enter** after Submitted:

Class

Assignment

Due Date

Complete

Submitted

Use the **Insert Below** command on the Layout tab in the Insert group to add nine more rows of table cells.

g. Select the first row of table cells with the column headings, and change the font to **Bold** and **Italic**, and the font size to **16 pt**. Widen columns as needed. Select all remaining cells below the first row, and change the font size to **12 pt**. You should have ten rows below the title row, which makes a total of eleven rows.

h. Maximize your OneNote screen. Place the pointer on the right edge of the table border to display a left and right pointing arrow. Drag the edge to the right until all table headings are on a single line.

> **TROUBLESHOOTING:** Depending on which edge you place the pointer, the double arrow will be white with a black outline or black with two vertical lines between the arrows. Place the pointer on the edge that has the black double arrow with two vertical lines between the arrows.

i. Click the **Insert tab**, and click the **Page Templates button** in the Pages group. Click **Save current page as a template** at the bottom of the Templates pane. Type **Assignments** in the Template name text box in the Save As Template dialog box, and click **Save**. Close the Templates pane.

j. Click in the first cell below the Class heading. Type **Macro Economics**, and press **Tab**. Type **Read Chapters 1–3. Answer questions at the end of each chapter.** Press **Tab**, and type **September 4, 2019**. Resize columns as needed to display contents.

STEP 2 » USE LINKS TO ADD A TABLE OF CONTENTS TO A NOTEBOOK

Bonnie occasionally has trouble finding the exact section she needs when it is time to review her course notes. Her professor suggested using a table of contents section to help her more easily locate content for which she is searching. Refer to Figure 2.15 as you complete Step 2.

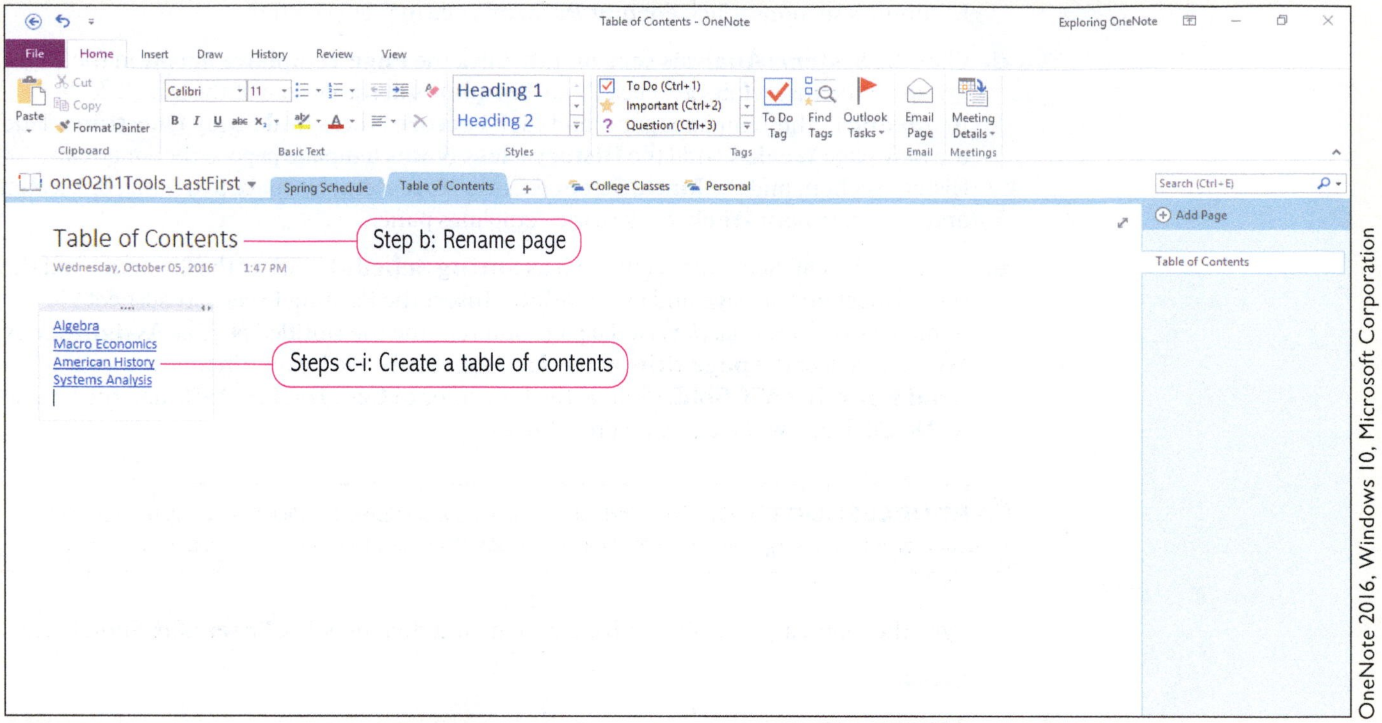

FIGURE 2.15 Linked Content

a. Add a new section to the one02h1Tools_LastFirst notebook. Rename the section **Table of Contents**.

b. Name the default page **Table of Contents**.

c. Type **Algebra** at the left margin below the date inserted into the page and press **Enter.**

d. Type **Macro Economics** and press **Enter**.

e. Double-click the word **Algebra** to select it. Click Link in the Links group on the Insert tab. Expand the one02h1Tools_LastFirst notebook, select the **Algebra section**, and then click **OK**.

f. Create a link to the **Macro Economics section** using the method in Step e. Ensure the insertion point moves to the next line.

g. Right-click on the **American History section tab** and click **Copy Link to Section.**

h. Click the line below Macro Economics, click the Home tab, and click **Paste** in the Clipboard group. Press **Enter**.

i. Type **[[Systems Analysis]]** and press **Enter**. Remember, the dotted line indicates a page or section that is empty.

STEP 3 » CHECK SPELLING, USE A THESAURUS, AND RESEARCH A TOPIC

To make sure she has not inadvertently added spelling mistakes to her notebook, Bonnie asked you to help her check spelling. She would also like to use the thesaurus to replace a word and research a topic using the research tools built into OneNote. Refer to Figure 2.16 as you complete Step 3.

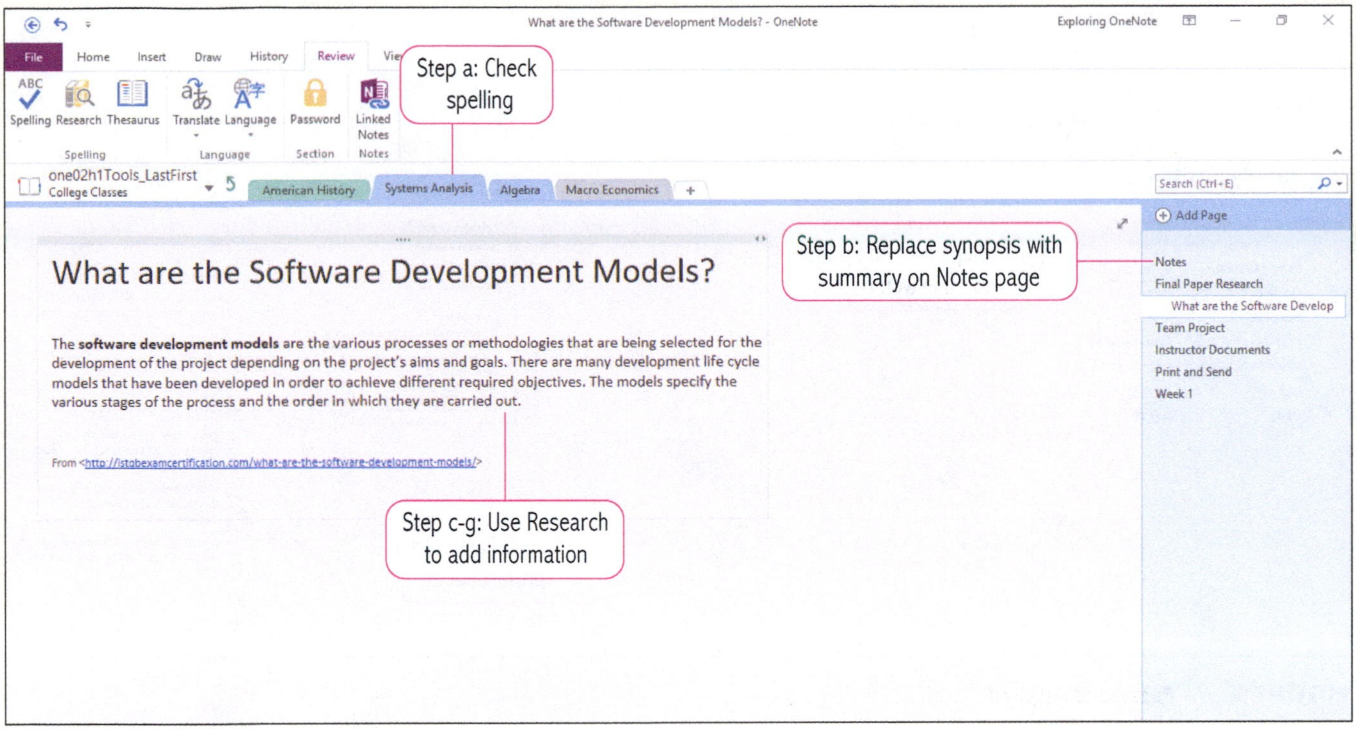

OneNote 2016, Windows 10, Microsoft Corporation

FIGURE 2.16 Research in OneNote

a. Navigate to the **Systems Analysis section Notes page**. Click the **Review tab**, and click **Spelling** in the Spelling group to check the spelling in the Systems Analysis section. Ignore the word *Abend* if it is noted as misspelled. Accept all other corrections.

b. Select the word **synopsis** on the Systems Analysis section Team Project page, and click **Thesaurus** in the Spelling group. Find *summary* in the Thesaurus pane in the list of suggested words. Click the **arrow** and click **Insert**. Close the Thesaurus pane.

c. Click **Research** in the Spelling group, and type **software development models** in the Search for text box. Click the **Bing arrow**, below the *Search for* text box, and select **All Research Sites**.

d. Click the **hyperlink** below any one of the search return items, avoiding all Wikipedia.org listings. Maximize the browser. Select the **title and first paragraph of text** and press **Ctrl+C** to copy the text.

e. Click the **Show hidden icons arrow** in the system tray, and click the **New quick note icon**. Click on the **Quick Note screen** and press **Ctrl+V** to paste the copied text into Quick Notes. Close Quick Notes.

f. Click the **Notebook pane tab** (the arrow to the left of the first section tab), in OneNote. Scroll to the bottom of the notebook file list as necessary and click **Quick Notes**. Right-click on the tab for the page you just copied into Quick Notes. Click **Move or Copy**. Expand the **one02h1Tools_LastFirst notebook**, expand the **College Classes group section**, and click **Systems Analysis**. Click **Move**.

g. Navigate to the Systems Analysis section. Drag the new page tab to move the page below the Final Paper Research page. Right-click the tab, and click **Make Subpage**. Close the Research pane.

Bonnie wants to add some personal information to her notebook. After she creates the Personal section, she asks you to help her password protect the section containing her personal information. Refer to Figure 2.17 as you complete Step 4.

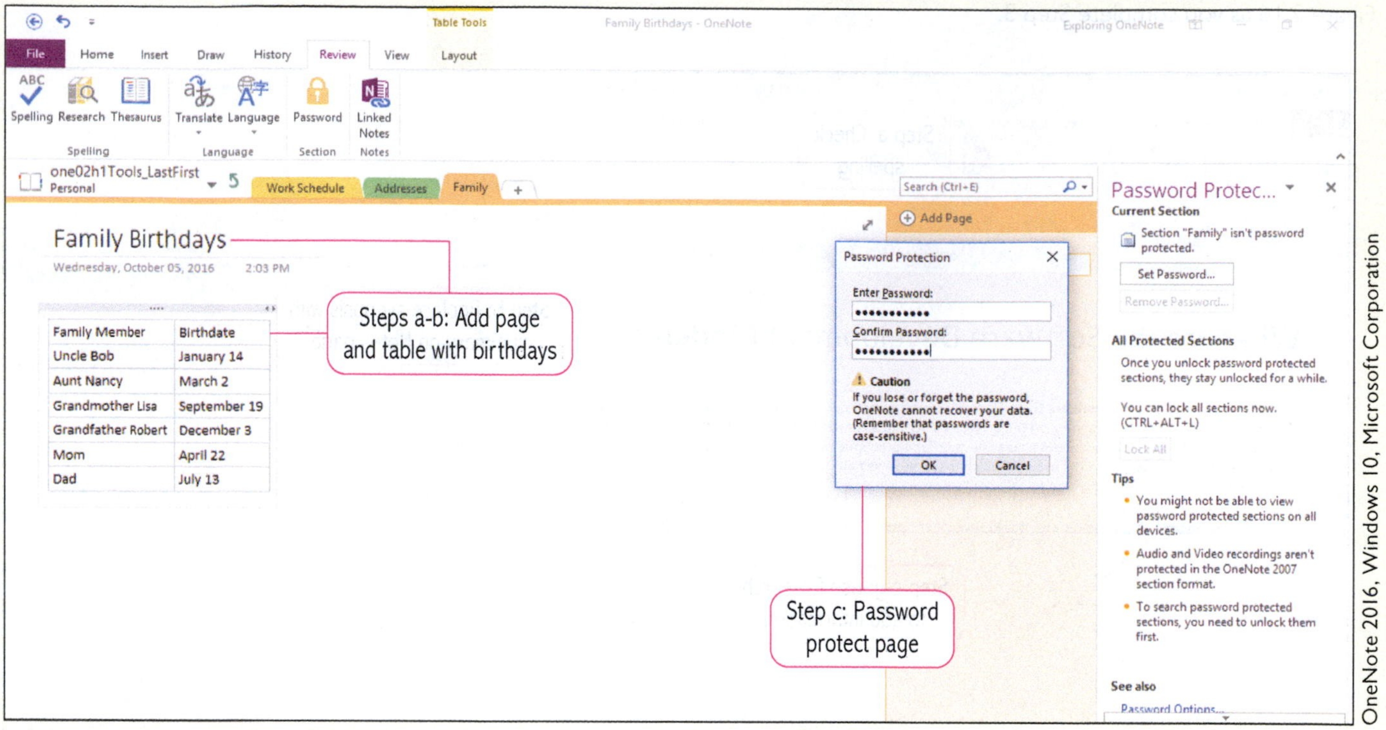

FIGURE 2.17 Password Applied

a. Add a new section titled **Family** in the Personal section group. Name the Untitled page as **Family Birthdays**.

b. Type **Family Member** on the Family Birthdays page below the date, press **Tab** and then type **Birthdate**. Press **Enter**. Type **Uncle Bob**, press **Tab**, type **January 14**, and then press **Enter**. Type **Aunt Nancy**, press **Tab**, and then type **March 2**. Continue to add the following information to the table:

Grandmother Lisa	**September 19**
Grandfather Robert	**December 3**
Mom	**April 22**
Dad	**July 13**

c. Click **Password** in the Section group on the Review tab, and click **Set Password** in the Password Protection pane. Type **OneNote2016** in the Enter Password text box, in the Password Protection dialog box, press **Tab**, and then retype **OneNote2016** in the Confirm Password text box. Click **OK**. Close the Password Protection pane.

With exams coming up, Bonnie has been reviewing her notes. She has decided to add tags to material the instructors have indicated will be on the tests, and wants to mark topics she needs help understanding. Refer to Figure 2.18 as you complete Step 5.

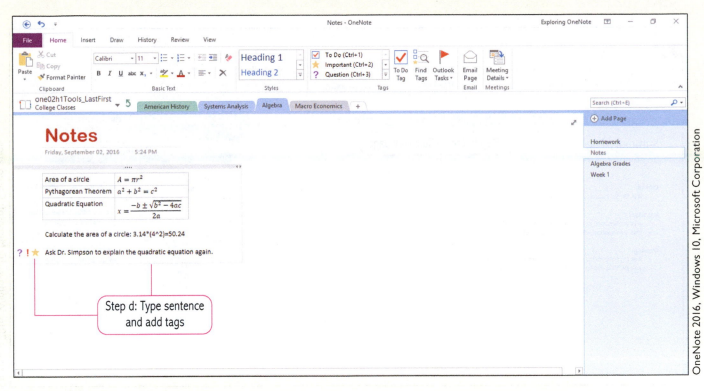

FIGURE 2.18 Tags Applied

a. Click the green **Navigate to parent section group arrow**. Select **all cells** below the Complete and Submitted headings on the Spring Schedule section tab Assignments Week 1 page. Click the **To Do Tag** in the Tags group on the Home tab to Insert the tag in all the cells below Complete and Submitted.

b. Click the **Page Templates button** in the Pages group on the Insert tab. Click **Assignments** below My Templates in the Templates pane to add two more Assignments Week 1 pages in the Weekly Assignments section. Change the **week number** for each inserted page until you have pages for Assignments Week 1 through Assignments Week 3. Close the Templates pane.

As the semester progresses, Bonnie can add a new Assignments page for each week.

c. Click the **Assignments Week 1 page tab**, and click the **To Do tag check boxes** on the first row below the table headings row in the Complete and Submitted columns to indicate that this assignment has been completed and submitted.

d. Navigate to the **Algebra section Notes page** in the College Classes section group. Below the calculation, type **Ask Dr. Simpson to explain the quadratic equation again.** Click before Ask in the sentence you just typed, and click **Question (Ctrl+3)** in the Tags group on the Home tab. Click **More** on the Tags gallery, and insert the **Critical tag**. Add an **Important tag** to indicate that this information will be on the exam.

STEP 6 » SEARCH FOR CONTENT IN NOTES, AND SEARCH FOR TAGS

Bonnie needs to locate her notes on the quadratic equation, and also needs to locate the Important tags in her notebook to help her know what specific information to study. You will show her how to search her notes for specific information and tags. Refer to Figure 2.19 as you complete Step 6.

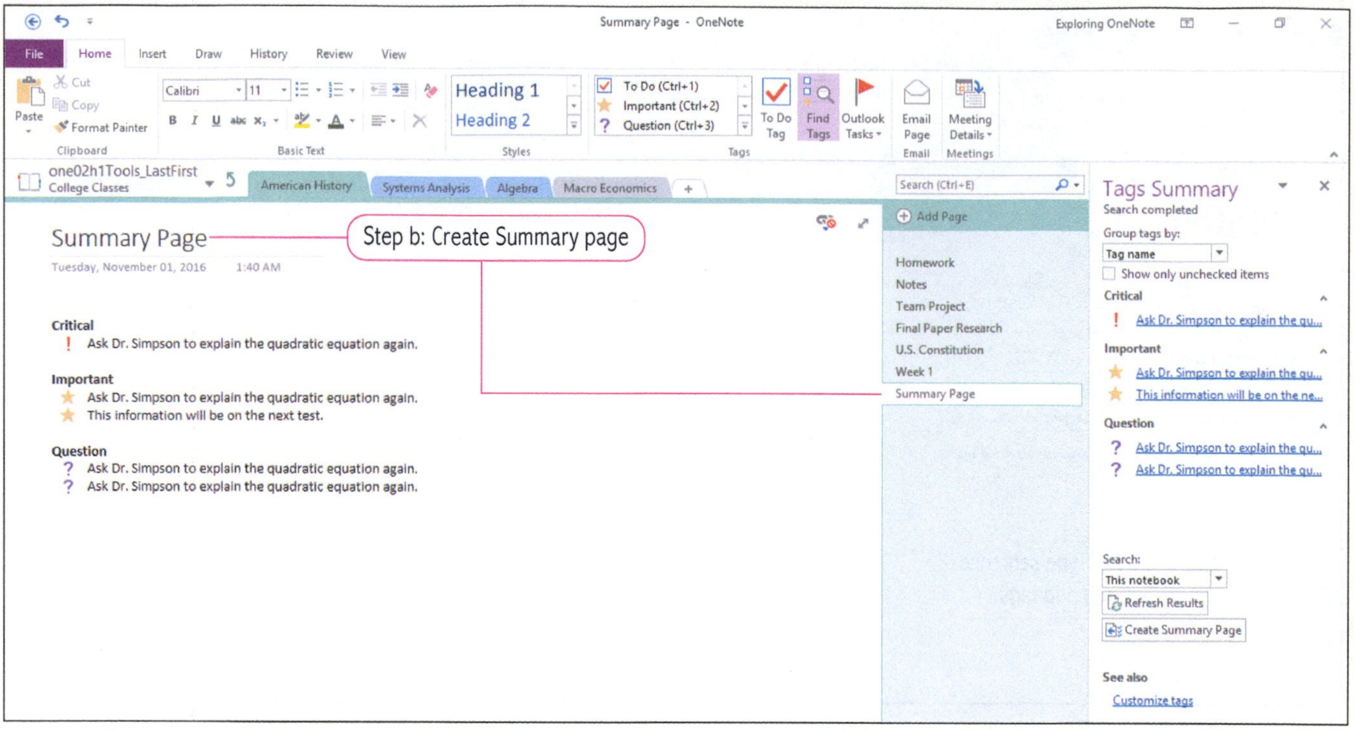

FIGURE 2.19 Summary Page

a. Navigate to the **Spring Schedule section tab**. Create a new section and name it **Screenshots**. Name the page as **Screenshots**. Click the **Macro Economics section tab** in the College Classes section group. Type **quadratic equation** in the Search box, and click the arrow at the far right of the Search box. Click **This Notebook** to set the search scope, and press **Enter**. Navigate to the **Algebra section Notes page**. Notice quadratic equation is highlighted. Press **Windows+PrtSrn** to take a screenshot. Navigate to the **Screenshots section tab**. Rename the page **OneNote Screenshots**. Paste the screenshot below the page title.

b. Click the **American History section Final Paper Research page tab** in the College Classes section group. Click **Find Tags** in the Tags group on the Home tab. Click the **arrow** below *Group tags by* in the Tags Summary pane and make sure **Tag name** is displayed. Select **This notebook** below Search. Click **Create Summary Page**. Rename the page **Summary Page**. Press **Windows+PrtSrn**. Navigate to the **Screenshots section tab** and paste the screenshot below the previous screenshot on the OneNote Screenshots page.

c. Export the notebook as **one02h1Tools_LastFirst.onepkg**. This file will be turned in at the end of the last Hands-On Exercise.

Collaboration with OneNote

Collaboration occurs when two or more people or organizations work together to complete a task or achieve a common goal. Examples of collaboration are students working to complete a group homework assignment, a work team creating an online store site, or an editorial team working with an author to complete a book.

In this section, you will learn about the collaboration tools available in OneNote. You will learn to create a notebook using OneNote Online, open the notebook in OneNote 2016 to insert content not available to you in the limited OneNote Online application, synchronize the notebook back to OneDrive, and share your notebook with a partner.

Working Online and Collaborating with OneNote

OneDrive is Microsoft's Web storage interface that also provides access to Word Online, Excel Online, PowerPoint Online, and OneNote Online to people with a Microsoft account. These *Online apps* are similar to the desktop versions, but have limited functionality. For example, in OneNote 2016, you can record an audio file from within OneNote. In OneNote Online, you can insert or embed an audio recording, but you cannot create one.

You can access OneDrive through any browser or from the Windows 10 menu. By default, the OneDrive app is installed with Windows 10. You may have to log in to OneDrive the first time you use the OneDrive app, but after that, Windows 10 will automatically sign into OneDrive when you turn on the computer and the Windows operating system loads. If the OneDrive tile is not on your Start screen, scroll down the Windows 10 menu list of available apps, right-click on the OneDrive listing, and then click Pin to Start.

TIP: TO ACCESS ONEDRIVE

To access OneDrive, you must have a Microsoft account. If you do not have a Microsoft account, you can set up a free account at:

- www.live.com
- www.outlook.com
- www.onedrive.com

Use OneNote Online

STEP 1 ❱❱ *OneNote Online* integrates seamlessly with OneNote 2016. By saving your OneNote 2016 notebook on OneDrive, you ensure that you have access to your notebooks from any location with Internet access. This is particularly helpful for students and professionals alike, because you no longer have to carry your notes with you. With access to an Internet-connected device, you have access to your notes.

The OneNote Online interface differs from the OneNote 2016 desktop interface as shown in Figure 2.20. In OneNote Online, if the Ribbon is minimized, click the HOME, INSERT, or VIEW tab, and then click the pin to keep the Ribbon open. Both versions have File, Home, Insert, and View tabs, but the Online version does not offer Draw, History, and Review. The Navigation Pane on the left contains all section and page tabs. There are no tabs on the right side of the screen.

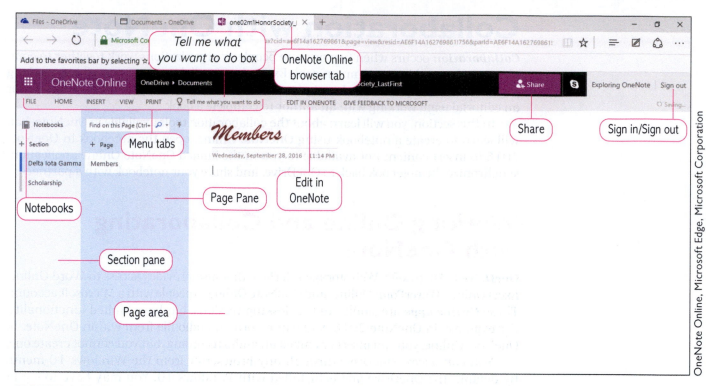

FIGURE 2.20 The OneNote Online Interface

The Section pane is on the far left side of the screen. Just to the right of the Section pane is the Page pane. The Ribbon is hidden until you click on the HOME, INSERT, or VIEW tabs. The FILE tab opens Backstage view, and the EDIT IN ONENOTE link opens the current Online App notebook in your desktop OneNote 2016 (see Figure 2.20). The *Tell me what you want to do* link helps you discover how to complete different actions in OneNote Online. The Share and Skype buttons may also appear at the top of your screen, depending on how your computer is configured. Share enables users to send an invitation to other people to offer them access to the notebook. Using the Skype button, you can use Voice over Internet Protocol (VoIP) to call others with a Skype account over the Internet.

> **TIP: FEEDBACK TO MICROSOFT**
> When you click the GIVE FEEDBACK TO MICROSOFT link, a Feedback window opens with three options, I like something, I dislike something, and I have a suggestion. The Privacy Statement link takes you to an online page where Microsoft explains how they collect and use personal data.

Basic OneNote functions are available in OneNote Online, too, but may work in a slightly different manner. For instance, you would use the +Section command at the top of the section tabs to add a section. Alternatively, you can either right-click an existing section tab and click New Section, or on the INSERT tab, in the Notebook group, click New Section. To add a new page, click the + Page command above the page tabs, or right-click on an existing section tab or page tab, and click New Page. As an alternative, you can click New Page in the Notebook group on the INSERT tab. To name a New Section 1 tab or to rename a section tab to another name, right-click on the tab and click Rename. To name an untitled page, click in the page title and type the title. This is the default page title.

To access only the files on OneDrive, locate the OneDrive link in the Apps menu. If you have not accessed OneDrive previously, or if you have not logged into your Microsoft account, you will be presented with a login screen. Type your Microsoft account e-mail and password, and then click Sign in.

Create a Notebook with Sections and Pages in OneNote Online

To use the Online apps, you will need to log in to your OneDrive account at www.onedrive.live.com (see Figure 2.21). When you access OneDrive, a list of folders will open. You will see a video link about OneDrive, two folders named Documents and Pictures, a PDF file titled Getting started with OneDrive, and a list of existing OneNote notebooks. Existing documents and spreadsheets will be located inside the Documents folder.

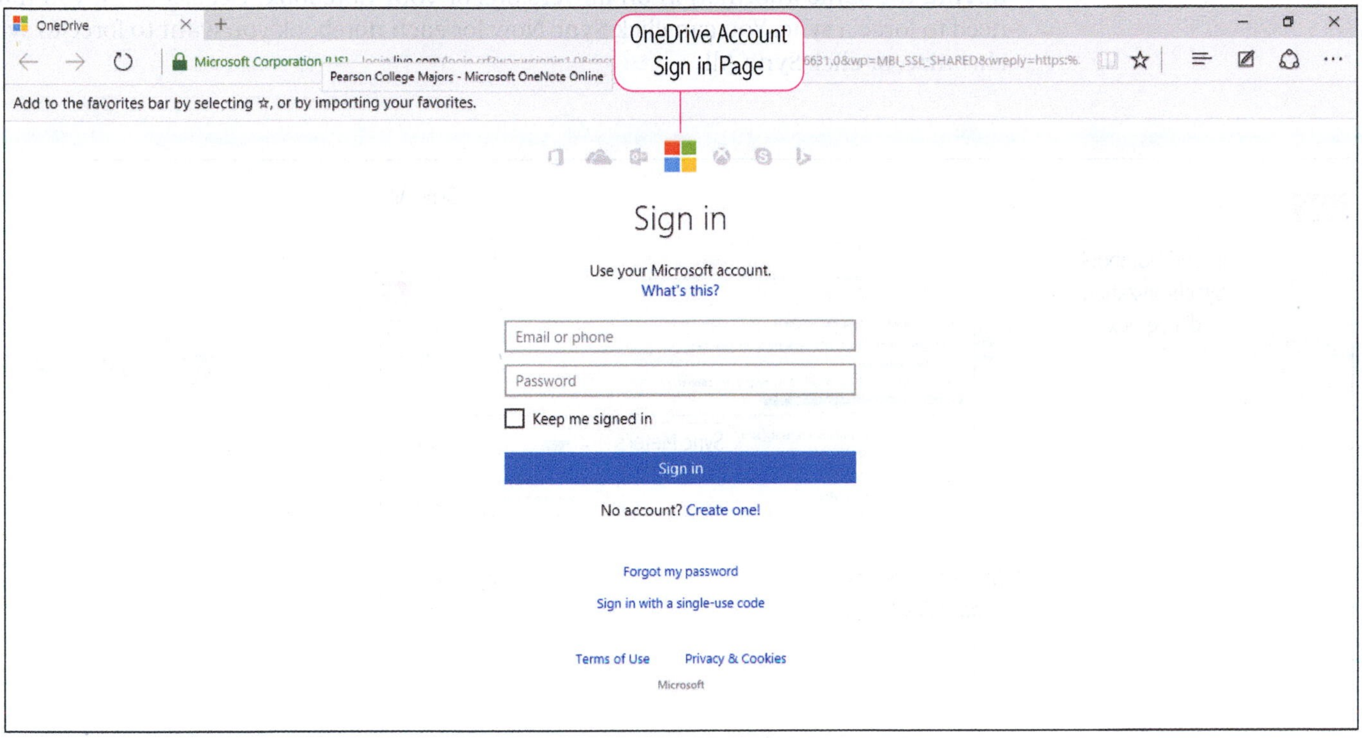

OneDrive, Microsoft Edge, Microsoft Corporation

FIGURE 2.21 OneDrive Account Sign-In Page

To create a notebook in OneNote Online, complete the following steps:

1. Click the +New arrow.
2. Click OneNote notebook.
3. Type a name for the new notebook in the Create New Notebook dialog box.
4. Click Create or press Enter.

When you first create a OneNote Online notebook, the notebook opens with one untitled section, which has one untitled page. To access an existing OneNote notebook in OneDrive, click the filename of the notebook. Each new notebook will have an Untitled Section and one Untitled Page. To rename a section tab in OneNote Online, right-click the section tab, click Rename, type the new section name, and then click OK. To rename a page, select the title on the page, press Delete, and type the new page title.

You cannot upload a file to a page in OneNote Online. However, you can use the EDIT IN ONENOTE tab to open the Online App notebook in your desktop OneNote 2016 application. At this point, you have the full capability of the desktop version for the notebook. Make the changes you need and sync the notebook to save those changes to the OneDrive notebook. To close the OneNote Online app, click Sign out in the top right corner of the app screen.

Synchronize OneNote 2016 with OneNote Online

STEP 2 》》 To save changes made in your OneNote Online notebook to your desktop notebook, you *sync* the two to make them the same. Syncing is done from within OneNote 2016, so you will have to click Edit in OneNote to open the OneNote Online notebook in OneNote 2016. Click Yes when asked if you want to change apps. Click Yes in the Microsoft OneNote Security Notice dialog box. Navigate to Backstage view and click View Sync Status. The Shared Notebook Synchronization dialog box displays (see Figure 2.22). At the top of the dialog box, you have the option to Sync automatically whenever there are changes or Sync manually. If you sync automatically, you never have to worry about not having the same information on all versions of your notebook. Occasionally, you may need to force a sync. You can click Sync Now for each notebook you want to force to synchronize, or click Sync All.

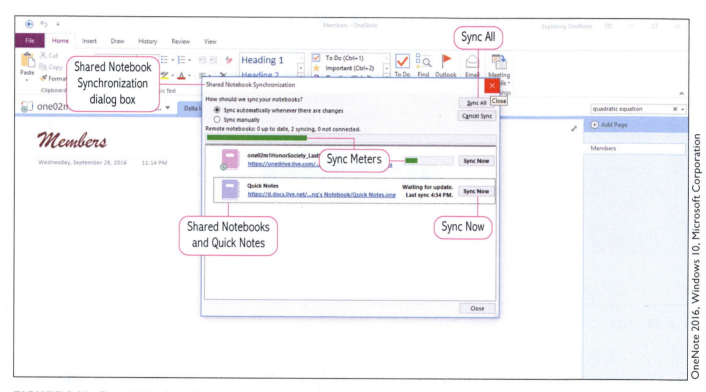

FIGURE 2.22 Shared Notebook Synchronization Dialog Box

Share a Notebook

STEP 3 》》 OneNote notebooks can be shared with anyone with OneNote or the OneNote Online App access, even if they are using iOS or Android systems. The ability to *share* notebooks with fellow workers, students, or family is a powerful feature allowing teams or groups to collaborate on projects. Before you can share a OneNote notebook, it must have been created on OneDrive, or moved to OneDrive before sharing. For instance, opening a OneNote notebook saved to OneDrive during an online meeting via a chat using an application such as Skype, enables you to share the notebook with everyone in the meeting.

There are several options from which to select when you are sharing your notebook. From OneNote 2016, click the File tab, click Share in Backstage view, and select one of the sharing options, Share with People, Get a Sharing Link, or Share with Meeting (see Figure 2.23). If the notebook is saved on your hard drive but not on OneDrive, you will need to put it on OneDrive to share it. To share your OneNote Online notebook, click + Share at the top right corner of the screen, and then select Invite People or Get a Link (see Figure 2.24).

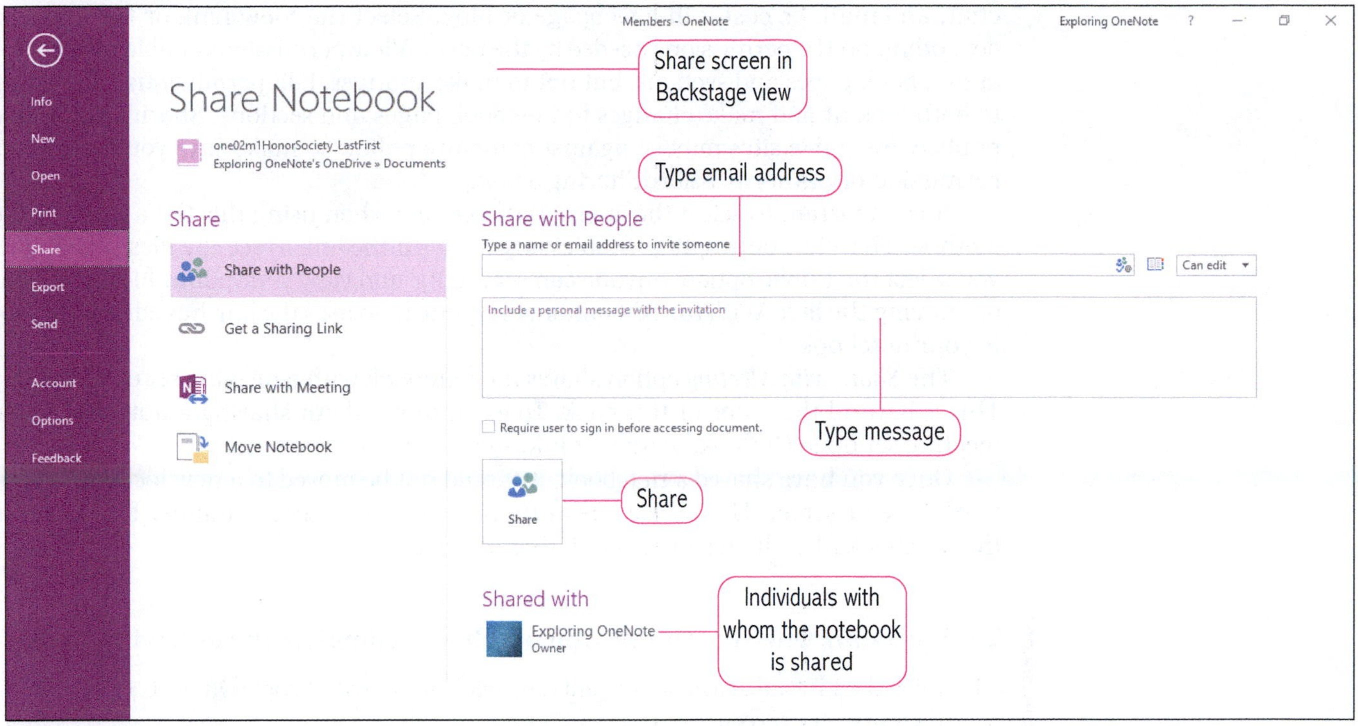

FIGURE 2.23 Sharing a Notebook in OneNote 2016

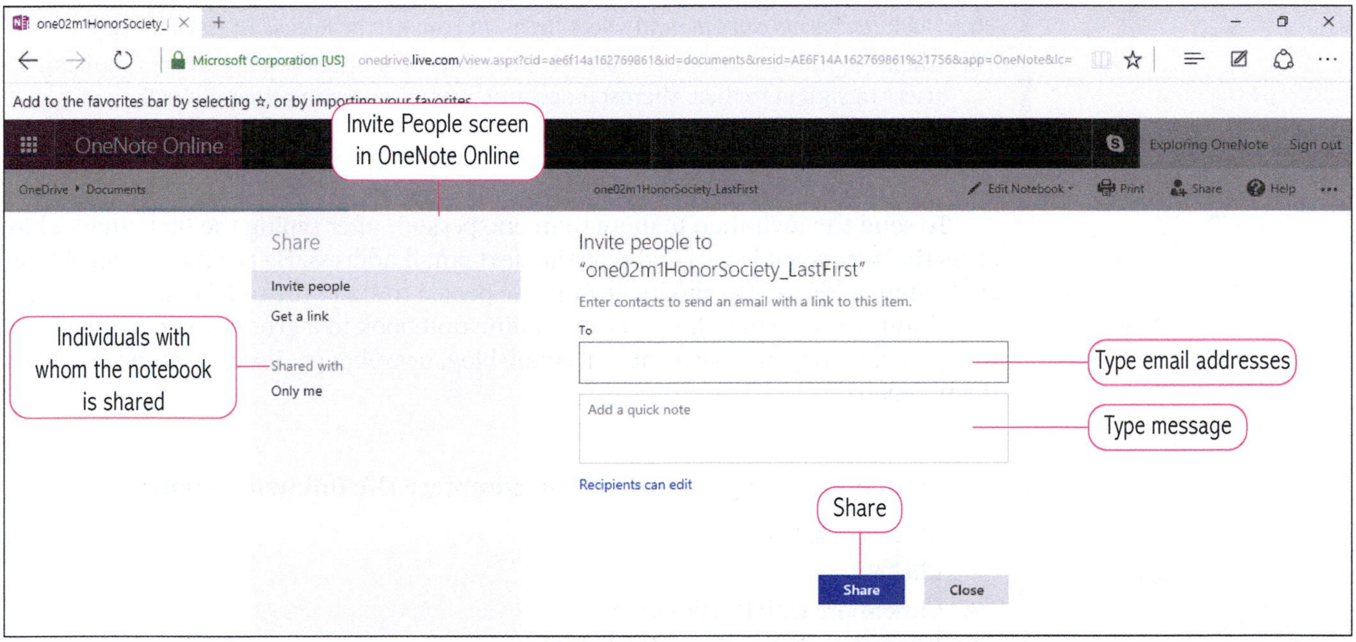

FIGURE 2.24 Sharing a Notebook in OneNote Online

Share with People enables you to send email to multiple individuals and select what permissions they have, either Can edit or Can view. Although you can select multiple individuals, you can only select one permissions level. If you need some people to have the ability to edit the notebook, you will need to send more than one Share with People email. You can also choose whether users are required to log in with a Microsoft account. Note that if you choose this option, users without a Microsoft account will not be able to log in.

The *Get a Sharing Link* option enables you to get a link that can be shared with users on social networks, such as Twitter or Facebook. You can also send the link in an online chat, an email, or post it in a webpage or blog. Select the View Link or the Edit Link, depending on the permissions needed by the users. View permissions enable users to look at notebook pages and sections, but not to make changes. Edit permissions enable users to both look at and make changes to notebook pages and sections. Sharing the link on publicly available sites may be against company policy, so make sure you have proper permission or authority before Sharing a link.

It is important to select the appropriate options when using this Get a Sharing Link method. The View only option enables anyone with the link to see the files you share. If you select the Public option, anyone can search for and view your public files, even without having the link. With the Edit option, everyone who uses the link has edit permissions to your notebook.

The *Share with Meeting* option shares the notebook with a meeting set up in Outlook. This is beyond the scope of this book. To learn more about sharing a notebook with a meeting set up in Outlook, search for information in your browser.

Once you have shared a notebook, it should not be moved to a new location on your hard drive or server. This breaks the **path**, the route the user's computer follows to find the notebook file, which causes the share not to work.

To share your OneNote Online App notebook, complete the following steps:

1. Click the FILE tab, click Share, and then click Share with People OR click +Share at the top of the screen.
2. Ensure Invite people in the Share dialog box is selected.
3. Type an email address in the To text box.
4. Type a note in the *Add a quick note* text box.
5. Click *Recipients can edit*, and select *Recipients can edit* or *Recipients can only view*.
6. Click *Require user to sign in before accessing document* check box if you are requiring users to sign in to their Microsoft accounts before accessing the notebook.
7. Click Share.

To send the invitation to more than one person, after typing the first email address, press the semicolon key (;) and type the next email address. By typing a semicolon after each email address, you can invite multiple people to share the notebook.

If you want to share the OneNote Online notebook to a group, you can create a link that you can copy and paste into an email, blog, or webpage. Users click the link to open the notebook.

To create a link to open a notebook, complete the following steps:

1. Click the FILE tab.
2. Click Share.
3. Click Share with People button.
4. Select Get a link in the Share dialog box.
5. Select a sharing option:
   - View Only—enables person to view the notebook, but not make changes to it.
   - Edit—enables the person to make changes to the notebook.
6. Click Create link.
7. Copy the link.
8. Paste the link in the email, blog, or webpage.

Use Version Control and Track Multiple Authors

STEP 4 ›› In OneNote 2016, the History tab provides access to review all changes made to the notebook, even if those changes were made by someone else with whom you have shared the notebook. The Unread group contains commands to help you locate changes you have not yet seen, and then mark them as read. In the Authors group, Recent Edits enables you to check for changes made Today, Since Yesterday, Last 7 Days, and up to the Last 6 Months. This is really helpful if several people are working in the notebook and made changes that need to be reviewed. Using Find by Author, you can search through a section, a section group, a notebook, or even all notebooks to find changes made by a specific author. The Hide Authors command hides the author information. It is a toggle button, so to show the author information again, simply click the Hide Authors command again.

The History group contains the Page Versions and the Notebook Recycle Bin commands as shown in Figure 2.25. Once a version has been reviewed and approved, previous versions can be deleted using the Page Versions. The Notebook Recycle Bin holds all deleted pages, sections, and notebooks until the Recycle Bin is emptied, or for 60 days, whichever comes first. To move a page or section out of the Recycle Bin, right-click the page name, click Move or Copy, and move it to the notebook. You can completely disable history for a specific notebook by using either Page Versions or Notebook Recycle Bin commands. Disabling the history of a notebook means that OneNote will not keep a copy of deleted pages or sections. Because the Recycle Bin acts as a safety net that enables you to retrieve accidentally deleted pages and sections, you should consider very carefully before disabling the history.

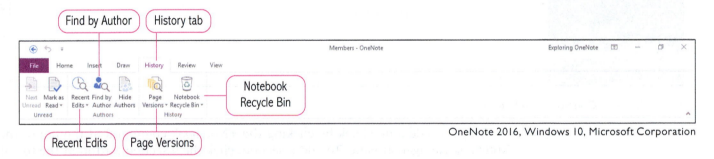

FIGURE 2.25 The History Tab

In OneNote Online, the History tab is not available. To see the versions and authors, you must use the View tab. The Page Versions command displays a list of all versions available in the Online App. Versions cannot be discarded in the Online App.

Use the OneNote App

STEP 5 ›› In addition to OneNote 2016 desktop application and OneDrive OneNote Online, there is a **OneNote app** installed by default in your Windows 10 device. You can access it in the apps list in the Start menu or through the Windows store if it is not on your device. The OneNote app is primarily designed for touch screens on tablets and smartphones. Ribbon tabs and commands are larger, because fingers will be utilized to navigate the screen and select commands. Through the OneNote app, you can access OneDrive OneNote Online to make quick additions to your notes pages, add new sections or pages, or even create a new notebook. When you sync the files, your changes are saved back to your OneNote Online notebook.

The first time OneNote app is used, you will have to set up the app. If you use the Express Set Up button, the app will access your system's OneNote 2016 application information to configure the app to work with your existing OneNote desktop installation. The user interface of the Online app is different from that of the desktop application. When the OneNote app opens, the most recently opened notebook displays open on the screen. Section tabs are above the page area. Pages for the open section are listed in the

Pages Pane on the left side of the screen. The + sign at the right end of the section tabs adds a new section. The + Page at the top of the Pages Pane adds a new page. The Show Navigation button opens the Navigation Pane as shown in Figure 2.26.

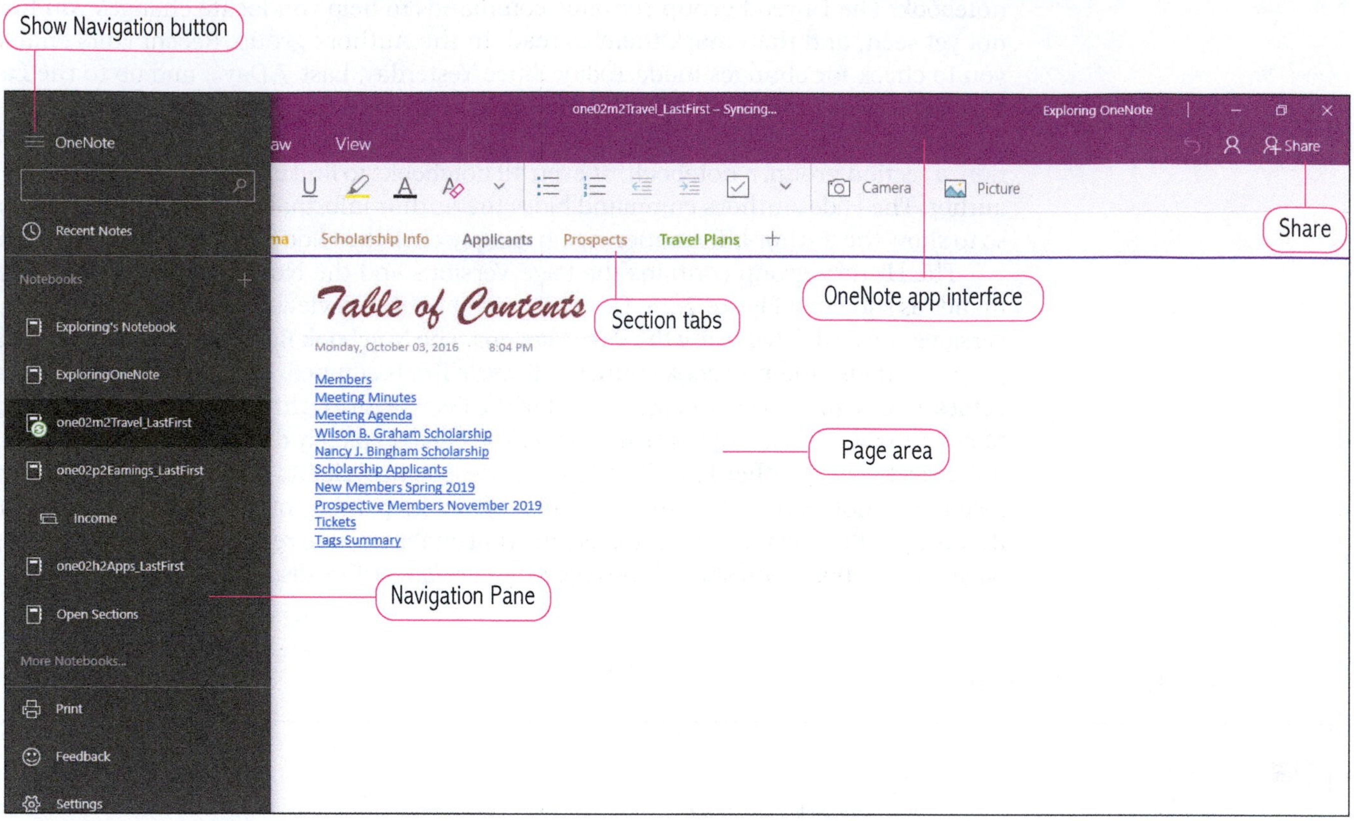

FIGURE 2.26 OneNote App Interface

You can add a notebook by clicking the +Notebook command at the top of the Notebook Navigation Pane. To add a section, click the +Section button at the top of the Section Pane, or click the + tab at the right of the section tabs. To add a page, click the +Page button at the top of the Page pane. To rename a section, right-click the current name. In the menu, select Rename Section. Other options available for working with sections in the menu include Delete Section, Move/Copy, Section Color, Copy Link to Section, Pin to Start, and Lock Protected Sections. Right-clicking a page name opens a menu with Delete Page, Rename Page, Subpages, Copy Link to Page, and Pin to Start buttons. However, to delete a notebook, you will need to use the desktop version or OneDrive Online.

To Insert content into a page, select the page, and click in the page where you want to add content or type. In the Windows 10 version of the OneNote app, the Ribbon is at the top, very similar to the Ribbon in OneNote Online. The Ribbon tabs are Home, Insert, Draw, and View. Inking is the method of using your finger or stylus to write notes into a page when using the OneNote app on a tablet or PC with a touch screen. The Draw tab provides access to commands used to change the ink color or line weight, or erase writing you have added to the page.

Quick Concepts

5. What is the advantage of syncing your online notebook with your desktop notebook? *p. 86*

6. What is the advantage of collaborating online with a team? *p. 83*

7. What are the permissions options you can select when sharing a notebook and when would you use each? *p. 88*

8. Explain the importance of versions and identifying authors of shared documents. *p. 89*

Hands-On Exercises

2 Collaboration with OneNote

Bonnie has decided to create a new OneNote notebook on OneDrive to keep notes for her personal life. After she gets started, she realizes that some of the features she wants to use are not available in OneNote Online, so she will have to open the Online notebook in the desktop application.

STEP 1 ›› **CREATING A ONENOTE ONLINE NOTEBOOK AND OPENING IT IN ONENOTE 2016**

Bonnie has asked you to help her create a new OneNote Online notebook for personal notes. Refer to Figure 2.27 as you complete Step 1.

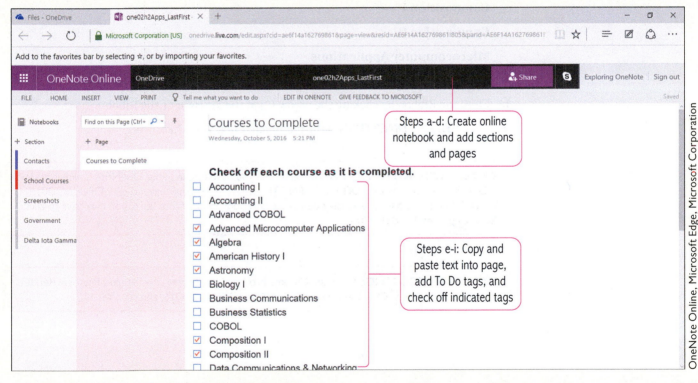

FIGURE 2.27 Create a OneNote Online Notebook

a. Navigate to **www.onedrive.com** in your browser. Ensure that you are signed in with your Microsoft account.

b. Click **+New** on the top menu bar. Click **OneNote notebook**. In the Create New Notebook dialog box, type **one02h2Apps_LastFirst** and click **Create**.

c. Ensure the browser window is maximized. Right-click the **Untitled section tab** on the left side of the screen in the Section pane, click **Rename**, type **Contacts**, and then click **OK**. Enter **Family Contacts** for the page title. Click **+Page** in the Page pane to add a page. Title the page **School Contacts**. Add a page in the Page pane. Title the new page **Job Search Contacts**.

d. Add a section in the Section pane. Title the section **School Courses**, and click **OK**. Title the page **Courses to Complete**, and press **Enter**.

e. Click below the date in the **Courses to Complete** page on the School Courses section. Open *one02h2List.docx* in Word. Press **Ctrl+A** to select all the text, right-click the selected text, and then click **Copy**. Close the Word document. Paste the copied list on the Courses to Complete page.

f. Click the **Home tab**. At the far right of the Ribbon, click the **Expand the Ribbon** tack icon to pin the Ribbon open.

g. Click to the left of Accounting 1 in the list, and press **Enter**. Move the insertion point to the blank line above Accounting 1. Type **Check off each course as it is completed**. Select the text and right-click the selected text. Change the font to **Bold** and **16 pt**.

h. Change the font size of the listed courses to **14 pt**. Click to the left of Accounting I, click the Tag button, and then click **To Do Tag** in the Tags group of the Home tab. Select the remaining course list, click the **Tag button**, and then click **To Do Tag** to add a check box before each of the courses listed.

i. Click the **check box** before the following courses to indicate they were completed:

Advanced Microcomputer Applications

Astronomy

Composition I

Composition II

Microcomputer Applications

Music Appreciation

j. Close the Ribbon by clicking the arrow (^) at the far right of the Ribbon.

k. Click **EDIT IN ONENOTE** on the menu bar. Click **Yes** twice.

TROUBLESHOOTING: If this is the first time you have opened your OneNote Online notebook in OneNote 2016 using the EDIT IN ONENOTE command, you may have to click OneNote 2016, and click OK. If you have previously opened the notebook in OneNote 2016, you may have to click Allow to proceed, and click Yes.

TROUBLESHOOTING: Using the Chrome browser? In Chrome, the External Protocol Request dialog box may display. Click Launch Application. Click OneNote 2016, and click Yes.

STEP 2 » SYNCHRONIZE ONENOTE AND ONENOTE ONLINE

Bonnie wants to make sure all the information she added to her notebook in OneNote 2016 is reflected in her OneNote Online notebook. She asks you to help her synchronize the two notebooks. Refer to Figure 2.28 as you complete Step 2.

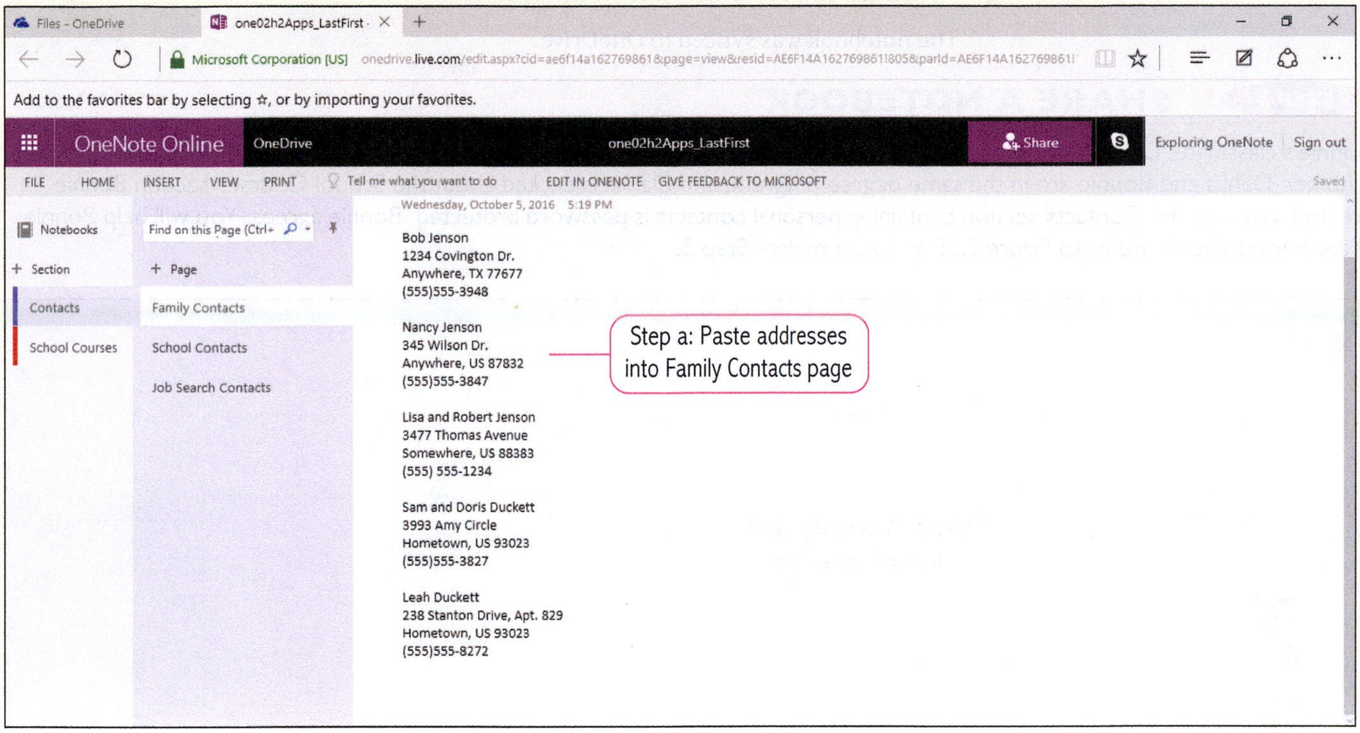

OneNote Online, Microsoft Edge, Microsoft Corporation

FIGURE 2.28 Content Synced to OneNote Online

a. Click on the **Contacts section tab** in OneNote 2016. Select the **Family Contacts page**, and wait until the page syncs. Open *one02h2Addresses.docx* in Word. Press **Ctrl+A** to select all the text, right-click the selected text, and then click **Copy**. Paste the copied list of addresses on the Family Contacts page. Close the Word document.

b. Click **File** to open Backstage view in OneNote 2016. Click the **View Sync Status button** to the right of the notebook list.

c. Click **Sync Now** to the right of the one02h2Apps_LastFirst notebook. Close the Shared Notebook Synchronization dialog box.

> **TROUBLESHOOTING:** If *Sync automatically whenever there are changes* is selected in the View Sync Status window, OneNote may have already synced the notebook. In this case, nothing observable will occur.

d. Close OneNote 2016.

e. Navigate to OneDrive in your browser.

> **TROUBLESHOOTING:** If the OneNote Online App is not open, in the Documents folder, locate the one02h2Apps_LastFirst OneNote file and double-click the filename to open the notebook.

f. Navigate to the Contacts section and click on the **Family Contacts page tab** in the one02h2Apps_LastFirst OneNote Online notebook.

Content added from the desktop application has been synchronized, or copied, to OneNote Online.

> **TROUBLESHOOTING:** If the Family Contacts page is blank, wait a few minutes. The addresses will display when syncing is complete.

g. Click **Sign out** at the far right of the menu bar.

The notebook was synced to OneDrive.

STEP 3 » SHARE A NOTEBOOK

Bonnie's classmate, Dahlia Washington, is impressed with Bonnie's contacts notebook. She asked Bonnie to share the notebook with her. Dahlia and Bonnie are in the same degree program, and Dahlia is excited about the School Courses section Bonnie created. Because the Contacts section containing personal contacts is password protected, Bonnie agrees. You will help Bonnie share her notebook. Refer to Figure 2.29 as you complete Step 3.

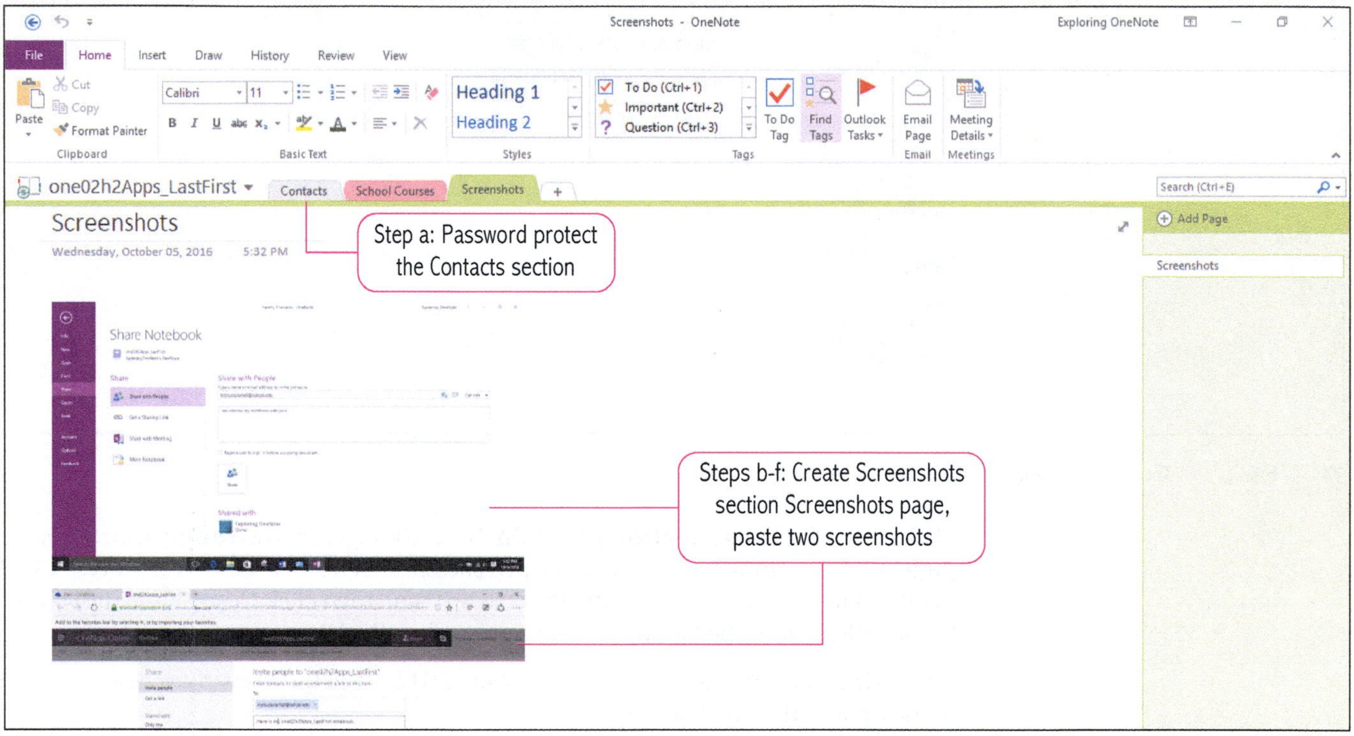

OneNote 2016, Windows 10, Microsoft Corporation

FIGURE 2.29 Screenshots of Share Settings

a. Open the one02h2Apps_LastFirst notebook in OneNote 2016.

b. Click the **Contacts section tab**. Click **Password** in the Section group on the Review tab. Click **Set Password**. Type **OneNote2016** in the Enter Password box. Press Tab and type **OneNote2016** in the Confirm Password box. Click **OK**. Close the Password Protection pane.

c. Click **File** in OneNote 2016. Click **Share**, and ensure Share with People is selected. Type **your instructor's email address** in the *Type a name or email address to invite someone* text box. Make sure **Can edit** is selected. In the personal message text box, type **I am sharing my notebook with you.**

d. Maximize the window. Take a screenshot of the screen. Do NOT click the Share button. Click **Back** to return to the notebook. Add a section titled **Screenshots**, and name the untitled page **Screenshots**. Paste the screenshot image in the Screenshots section Screenshots page. Sync and close OneNote 2016.

e. Open your one02h2Apps_LastFirst notebook in OneDrive, and ignore the password-protected section. Click the **Screenshots section** in the Section Navigation Pane. Click **Share** at the top of the OneNote Online screen. Type **your instructor's email address** in the To text box. Type **Here is my one02h2Apps_LastFirst notebook.** in the message box.

f. Take a screenshot of the screen. Do not click **Share**. Paste the screenshot below the previous image in the Screenshots section Screenshots page. Resize the second screenshot to be about the same size as the first using one of the sizing handles. Click **Edit in OneNote**, and close one02h2Apps_LastFirst.

STEP 4 ▶▶ **USE VERSION CONTROL AND TRACK MULTIPLE AUTHORS**

Bonnie and her partner have decided to share their notebooks with each other to make it easier to share notes. Refer to Figure 2.30 as you complete Step 4.

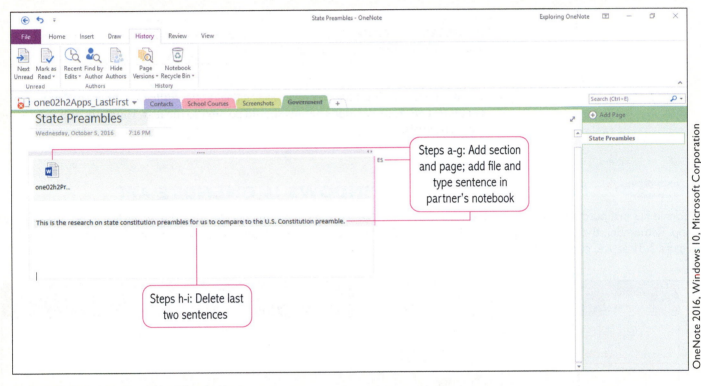

FIGURE 2.30 OneNote Identifies Authors

a. Open one02h2Apps_LastFirst in OneNote 2016. Share your one02 h2Apps_LastFirst notebook with your partner using the method practiced in Step 3. Make sure your partner has editing permission. Close one02h2Apps_LastFirst.

b. Open your email application. Locate your partner's email notifying you that the notebook is shared. Click **View in OneDrive**. Ensure you are signed in, and click **EDIT IN ONENOTE**. Click **Yes** when the *Did you mean to switch apps?* dialog box appears. Click **Yes** when the Microsoft OneNote Security Notice displays. Click the screen when *"You've turned off the option to sync your notebooks automatically. Tap or click here to sync this notebook now."* displays.

c. Click the **Password Protection notice**, and type **OneNote2016** in the Password Protection dialog box. Add a new section titled **Government**. Name the untitled page **State Preambles**. Press **Enter**.

d. Click **File Attachment** in the Files group on the Insert tab. Navigate to your student data files, and select *one02h2Preambles.docx*. Click **Insert**, and select **Attach File**.

e. Type the following sentence below the attached file: **This is the research on state constitution preambles for us to compare to the U.S. Constitution preamble.** Press **Enter** twice.

f. Type **Let's get together next week to finalize the outline for our paper.** Press **Enter**. Type **This project isn't fun at all.**

g. Click the **File tab**, ensure Info is selected in the left menu, and click the **View Sync Status button**. Click the **Sync Now button** to the right of the notebook name, wait until the sync completes, and then close your partner's notebook.

h. Open your own one02h2Apps_LastFirst notebook on OneDrive. Click the **View tab**, and click **Show Authors** in the Authors group.

Notice your partner's initials on the Government section State Preambles page.

> **TROUBLESHOOTING:** If your partner's initials are not showing, make sure your partner has completed the previous step, then try again.

i. Locate the text *Let's get together next week to finalize the outline for our paper. This project isn't fun at all.* Your partner's initials should be next to the text. Highlight and delete these two sentences.

Close OneDrive.

STEP 5 ›› INTRODUCTION TO WINDOWS 10 ONENOTE APP

Bonnie has just purchased a new tablet. Because the tablet has a touch screen, she decided that she would like to use the OneNote app. Remember, the OneNote app is not the same as OneNote Online, which is the OneDrive version of the application. Refer to Figure 2.31 as you complete Step 5.

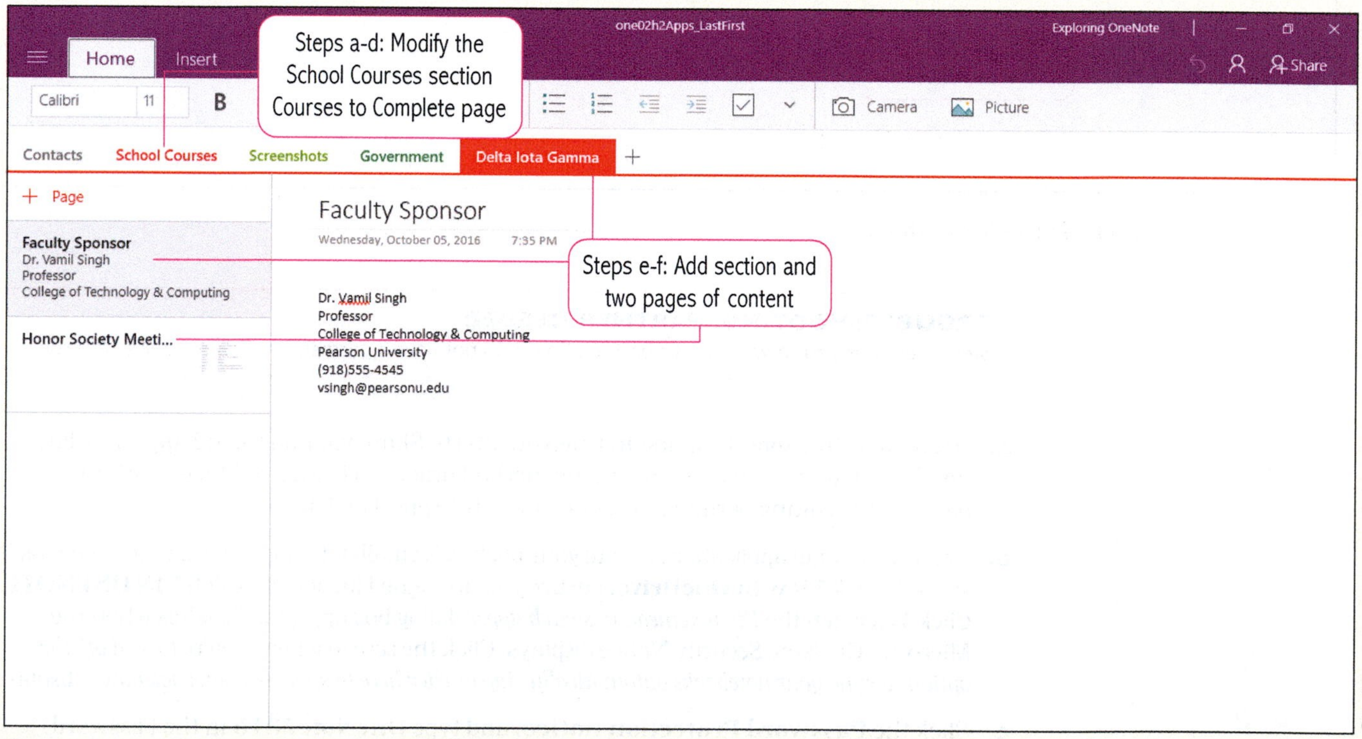

FIGURE 2.31 A Notebook in the OneNote App

OneNote App, Microsoft Corporation

a. Open the OneNote app from the Start menu. A blank OneNote pane opens.

> **TROUBLESHOOTING:** The OneNote app is installed in Windows 10 by default. You will find it on the Windows menu. Click Start, navigate to the O section of the menu, and then click OneNote. The desktop version of OneNote will be listed as OneNote 2016.
>
> If this is the first time the OneNote app has been used, click Use Express Settings in the Welcome to OneNote window. Click Recent Notes.
>
> If you have not logged into your Microsoft account, you may be required to do so.
>
> If you do not have the OneNote app installed on your PC, open the Windows Store. Search for OneNote, and install the app.

b. Click **Show Navigation** to the left of the Home tab. Locate and select the **one02h2Apps_LastFirst** notebook.

> **TROUBLESHOOTING:** If one02h2Apps_LastFirst is not listed in the Notebook Pane, click More Notebooks. Scroll until the file name displays, and click the file name.

c. Click the **School Courses section tab**. Click the **To Do Tag** before the following courses on the Courses to Complete page to indicate that these courses are completed:

Algebra

American History

Macro Economics

Speech Communication

d. Click after the end of the text on the Speech Communication line and press **Enter**. Type **Systems Analysis** and press **Enter**. Click the **check box** before Systems Analysis to indicate that this course is completed.

e. Click **+Section** to add a new section. Name the section **Delta Iota Gamma**. Rename the default page to **Faculty Sponsor**. Type the following information below the date, pressing **Enter** after each line:

Dr. Vamil Singh

Professor

College of Technology & Computing

Pearson University

(918)555-4545

vsingh@pearsonu.edu

f. Add a page titled **Honor Society Meeting Dates**. Click **File** on the Insert tab, and select **Insert PDF Printout**. Navigate to your student data files, select *one02h2Topics.pdf*, and then click **Open**. Scroll to the top of the notebook page.

g. Close the OneNote app. Open one02h2Apps_LastFirst in OneNote 2016. Sync the notebook. Verify the Delta Iota Gamma section and pages are present.

h. Export your notebook as **one02h2Apps_LastFirst.onepkg**.

i. Based on your instructor's directions, submit the following:

one02h1Tools_LastFirst.onepkg

one02h2Apps_LastFirst.onepkg

Chapter Objectives Review

After reading this chapter, you have accomplished the following objectives:

1. **Use tools and templates.**
   - Using the formatting commands on the Home tab, you can change text fonts, colors, and sizes. An easy way to change formatting throughout a document is to use the Format Painter in the Clipboard group on the Home tab.
   - Apply a page template: Page templates enable you to add a professionally designed page to your notebook.
   - Create a page template: An alternative to using a template from Microsoft is to create your own page template by designing the page, and saving it as a template using the *Save current page as a template* link at the bottom of the Templates pane.
   - Create a Wiki: Using links, a shared notebook can be used as a wiki. To create page links to other pages in a section, use the [[and]] brackets.
   - Use links to add a table of contents to a notebook: Because OneNote does not limit the number of sections and pages a notebook may contain, a table of contents makes it easier to locate specific sections or pages in a large notebook.
   - Convert handwritten notes created with pen and drawing tools to typed text: Though primarily designed for use with tablets, touch screens, or a stylus, the pen and drawing tools available on the Draw tab enable you to add your own artwork or write text onto a page. Notes taken using a stylus or finger can be converted to typed text.
   - Add rule lines: Rule lines make it much easier to keep notes straight on a touch device.
   - Check spelling, use a thesaurus, and research a topic: On the Review tab, you can check your spelling, use a thesaurus to find the right word, or research a topic online.
   - Apply a password: Password protection can be added to any section in a notebook. Once a section is password protected, you will need to enter the password to access the information.
   - Add tags: Tags help you indicate specific types of information in your notebook. Tags include To Do, Critical, Question, Important, and many more. These tags appear in the notebook as symbols.
   - Search notes: You can use the Search bar to search for a word or phrase in your notebook.
   - Find tags: The Find Tags command in the Tags group on the Home page locate information that has been tagged, and provides a summary of all tags in a notebook.

2. **Work Online and Collaborate with OneNote.**
   - Use OneNote Online: OneNote Online is available to anyone who has a Microsoft account, even if they do not own Microsoft Office 2016 or OneNote 2016. Although the interface differs, the way that OneNote Online works is very similar to that of the desktop application.
   - Create a notebook with sections and pages in OneNote Online: Using the OneDrive OneNote Online application, you can create notebooks with sections and pages. OneNote Online is a limited version of OneNote 2016.
   - Synchronize OneNote 2016 with OneNote Online: Using the Sync feature in OneNote enables you to have the same content notebook in all shared locations, including your desktop, OneDrive, or those with whom you have shared.
   - Share a notebook: Notebooks can be shared with instructors, family members, friends, or colleagues. When you share a notebook, you determine whether those with whom the notebook is shared can only view the notebook or if they can edit the notebook.
   - Use version control and track multiple authors: OneNote tracks authors of changes to a shared notebook and keeps track of versions of a notebook. This enables you to see what changes were made as well as who made them.
   - Use the OneNote app: The OneNote app is installed by default in Windows 10. This is the most limited version of OneNote, but it enables you to sync changes made in your notebook to OneDrive or your desktop.

Key Terms Matching

For each question, locate the term that best completes the sentence. Write the letter of the correct term in the blank:

a. Collaboration
b. Find Tags
c. Format Painter
d. OneDrive
e. OneNote 2016
f. OneNote app
g. OneNote Online
h. Online app
i. Page template
j. Pass phrase

k. Password protection
l. Path
m. Search term
n. Share
o. Sync
p. Tag
q. Templates pane
r. Toggle
s. Wiki

1. _____ The command that makes it easy to find marked content in a notebook. *p. 75*

2. _____ Microsoft's note taking software designed primarily for touch screen tablets and smartphones. *p. 89*

3. _____ An electronic marker inserted into a page to mark specific types of content. *p. 74*

4. _____ A command that is either on or off. *p. 74*

5. _____ A pre-designed format used for OneNote pages. *p. 64*

6. _____ A key word or group of words used to narrow down returned results. *p. 75*

7. _____ An action that makes a notebook the same on all platforms. *p. 86*

8. _____ The command that allows you to provide access to your OneNote notebooks to others. *p. 86*

9. _____ A group of words used as a password, or as the base for a password made up of the initials of the words. *p. 74*

10. _____ A tool that allows users to copy the formatting of one selection and paste it to another section. *p. 64*

11. _____ Contains a selection of pre-designed and formatted pages that can be inserted into a section. *p. 64*

12. _____ The version of the note taking software used in OneDrive. *p. 83*

13. _____ Limited function application available for use through OneDrive. *p. 83*

14. _____ An online storage platform that also provides access to limited versions of some web-based Microsoft Office applications. *p. 83*

15. _____ Prevents unauthorized individuals seeing or adding content to a section. *p. 71*

16. _____ Two or more groups or individuals working together on a common goal. *p. 83*

17. _____ Microsoft's note-taking application for the desktop environment. *p. 64*

18. _____ A shared electronic database or file with content that can be changed, added to, or deleted by anyone with whom it has been shared. *p. 66*

19. _____ The route a computer follows to find a file. *p. 88*

Multiple Choice

1. To copy the format of a section of text to another section, use the:
   - (a) Copy and Paste buttons
   - (b) Format Copy
   - (c) Format Painter
   - (d) Format dialog box

2. The commands on the _____ tab enable you to check versions and review who made changes to a shared notebook.
   - (a) View
   - (b) History
   - (c) Home
   - (d) Review

3. Which sharing option would be used to share your notebook on social media?
   - (a) Invite People
   - (b) Get a Sharing Link
   - (c) Share with Meeting
   - (d) Move Notebook

4. Which of the following is the best password?
   - (a) abcd1234
   - (b) redfern
   - (c) PWwiue35;k
   - (d) 1234546abc

5. To protect information in a section in your notebook, you can:
   - (a) Add password protection
   - (b) Delete the section
   - (c) Hide the section
   - (d) Move the section to OneDrive

6. Which of the following mistakes will the spelling checker *not* find?
   - (a) I senpt two nihts in London, England.
   - (b) Win I have enough thyme, I am taking a trip to France.
   - (c) The tour was overbookd and I had to wait in the bus station for three hours.
   - (d) The train was late getting to the stashun.

7. Which of the following is *not* available in OneDrive?
   - (a) OneNote Online
   - (b) Access Online
   - (c) Word Online
   - (d) PowerPoint Online

8. An easy way to add pre-designed page designs and formats to a OneNote notebook is to use a:
   - (a) Page form
   - (b) Section template
   - (c) Section form
   - (d) Page template

9. To Do, Contact, Important, and Idea are examples of:
   - (a) Tips
   - (b) Tags
   - (c) Notations
   - (d) Bookmarks

10. Which of the following is available for free through the Windows store?
    - (a) OneDrive
    - (b) OneNote App
    - (c) OneNote Online App
    - (d) OneNote 2016

Practice Exercises

1 Update an Existing Notebook

Janetta has decided to team up with two other sewing enthusiasts on her blog. She will be working with her sister, Megan, and her neighbor, Estela. Whereas she likes the notebook you created for her, she asked you to make some formatting changes. Refer to Figure 2.32 as you complete the exercise.

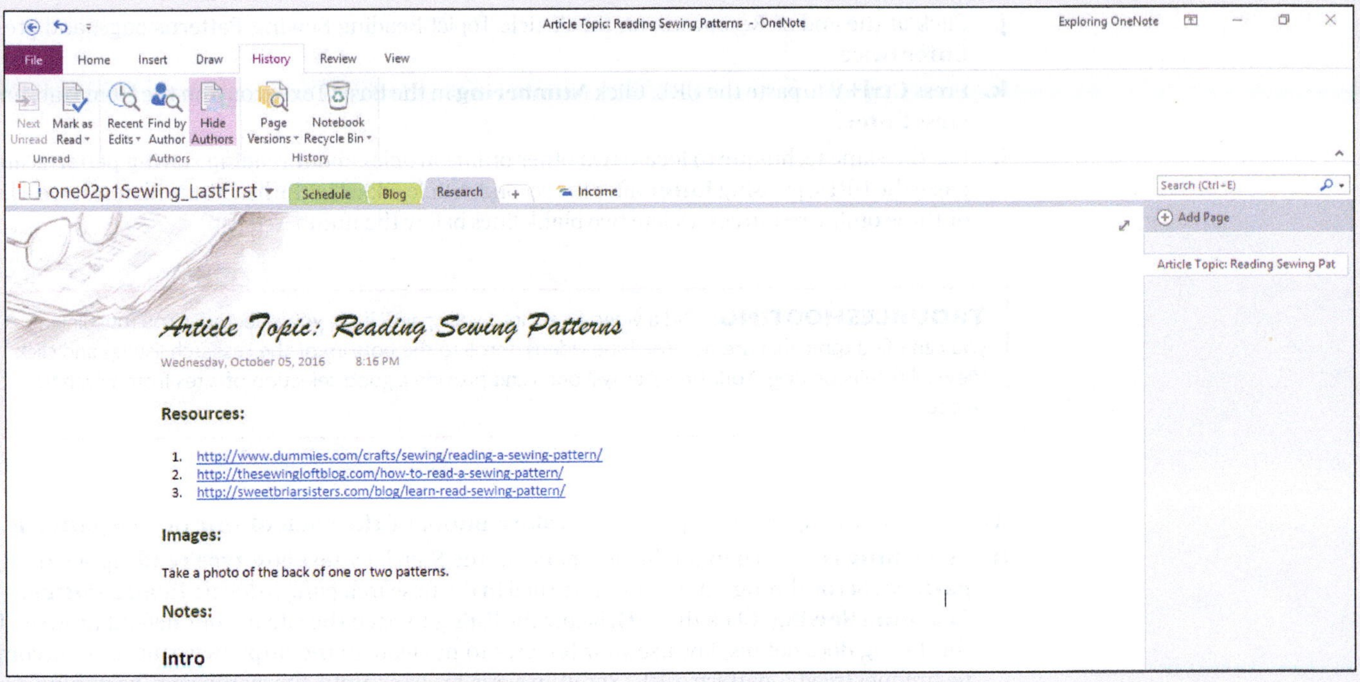

OneNote 2016, Windows 10, Microsoft Corporation

FIGURE 2.32 Formatted Blog Notebook

a. Unpack the *one02p1Sewing.onepkg* file, saving it as **one02p1Sewing_LastFirst**.

b. Click the **Income section group tab**. Click the **Applied Programs page tab** in the Affiliate Programs section. Select the page title, change the font to **Brush Script MT**, the font size to **26**, and the font color to **Green, Darker 50%**.

c. Select the **top table row contents**. Click **Bold** in the Basic Text group on the Home tab. Change the font size to **14 pt**.

d. Right-click the cell containing *Date Applied*, click **Table**, and then click **Insert Right**. Type **Commission**. Press **Tab** four times. Type **4%** and press **Tab** four times. Type **18%** and press the **down arrow** ↓. Type **10%**. Press the down arrow ↓. Type **8%**. Drag the right edge of the table to widen it until all first row text is on one line.

e. Click **Navigate to parent section group** (green arrow) to return to the main notebook. Add a section and name it **Research**. On the Insert tab, in the Pages group, add a **Glasses Corner template** from the Decorative category. Title the page **Article Topic:** (include the colon) and press **Enter**. Use Format Painter to copy the format from the Applied Programs page to the Article Topic: page.

f. Type **Resources:** (include the colon) below the date, and press **Enter** four times. Type **Images:** (include the colon) and press **Enter** four times.

g. Type **Notes:** (include the colon) and press **Enter** four times. Select **Resources:**. **Bold** the text, change font size to **14**, and change the color to **Green, Darker 50%**. Use Format Painter to change the font on Images: and Notes: to match Resources:.

h. Delete the **Untitled page**. Click **Page Templates** in the Pages group on the Insert tab. Click **Save current page as a template**. Type **Articles** in the Template name text box, and click **Save**. Close the Templates pane.

i. Change the title to **Article Topic: Reading Sewing Patterns**. Click the **Review tab**. Click **Research** in the Spelling group. Search for **reading sewing patterns** in the Research pane. Locate and click the **Reading a Sewing Pattern—dummies** URL in the Research pane (http://www.dummies.com/crafts/sewing/reading-a-sewing-pattern/). Copy the **URL** in the address box in your browser.

j. Click at the end of Resources: on the Article Topic: Reading Sewing Patterns page, and press **Enter** twice.

k. Press **Ctrl+V** to paste the URL. Click **Numbering** in the Basic Text group on the Home tab, and press **Enter**.

l. Use the same technique to locate two other online articles about reading sewing patterns and paste the URLs, pressing **Enter** after the second article added to the list. You will now have a list of three online resources. Delete two blank lines below the numbered list.

TROUBLESHOOTING: Did a video insert into your page? If so, you selected a YouTube link. If you can't find three that are not YouTube videos, scroll to the bottom of the research listings and click View all results on Bing. Your browser will open and provide a good selection of sites from which to select.

---

m. Click below Images: on the page. Type **Take a photo of the back of one or two patterns.**

n. Verify **Bing** is selected in the Review pane. In the *Search for* text box, type **reading a sewing pattern**. Scroll through the results returned in the Research pane to locate **Read a Pattern—Learning Sewing**. Click the **URL** below the listing to open the site in your default browser. If this listing does not display, use your browser to navigate to the http://www.burdastyle.com/techniques/read-a-pattern URL. Scroll in your browser until the paragraph beginning *Just starting to use patterns?* completely displays at the bottom of the screen. Click and drag to select the image through the end of the paragraph beginning *Just starting to use patterns?* Press **Ctrl+C**. Open **New quick note**. Paste the copied information into the Quick Note screen. Close Quick Note.

o. Display the one02p1Sewing_LastFirst notebook. Click **Quick Notes** in the Navigation Pane. Click the **Quick Notes page tab** that contains the content you just copied. Click the pattern image to select the container the content is in. Right-click the **top bar of the container** and click **Copy**.

p. Return to the Article Topic: Reading Sewing Patterns page. Click at the end of Notes and press **Enter** twice. Paste the copied container.

q. Close the Research pane. Click **Spelling** in the Spelling group on the Review tab.

r. Export the notebook as **one02p1Sewing_LastFirst.onepkg**. Close OneNote.

s. Based on your instructor's directions, submit one02p1Sewing_LastFirst.onepkg.

2 Create a Table of Contents, Password Protect a Section, Edit the Notebook in OneNote App

Janetta was able to make some changes in her notebook, but she would like to add a table of contents to help her navigate her notebook more quickly. She also thinks that the Earnings section in her notebook should not be available to her team. She has asked you to help her create a table of contents section and password protect the Earnings section. Refer to Figure 2.33 as you complete the exercise.

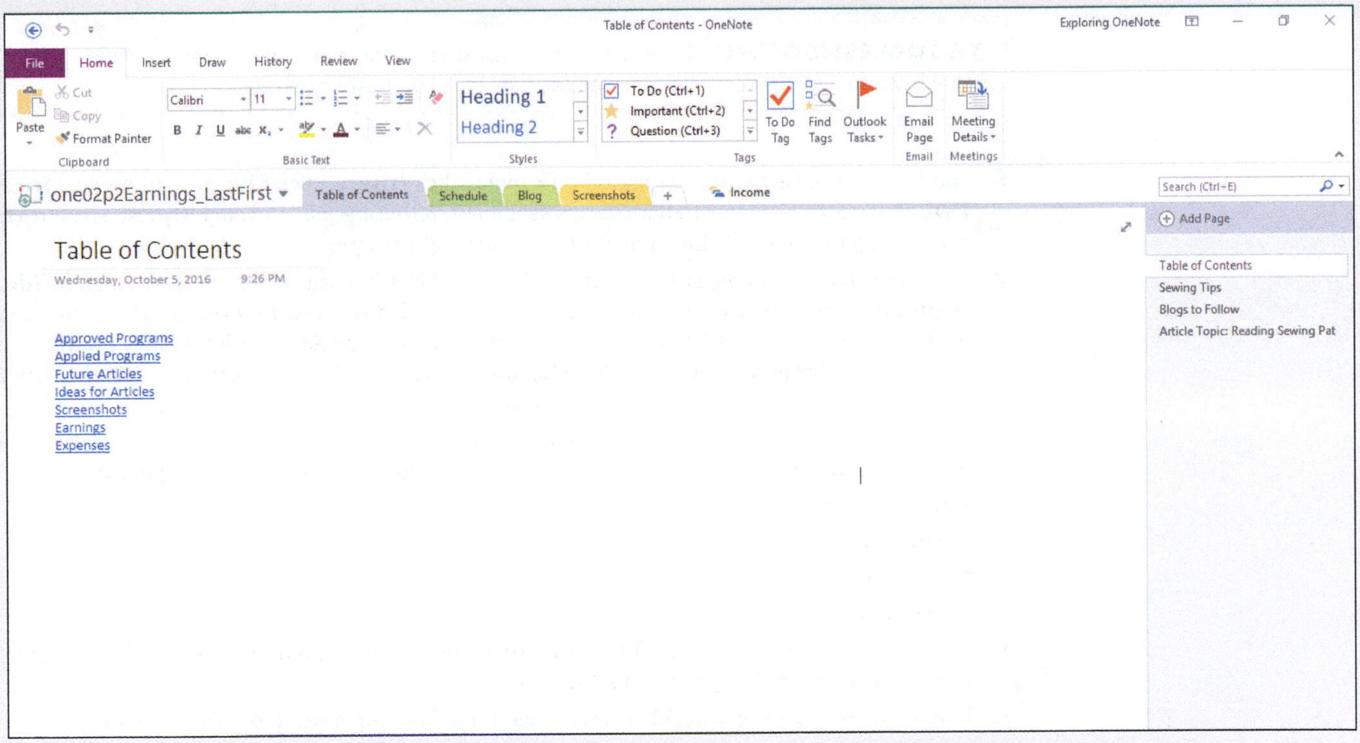

OneNote 2016, Windows 10, Microsoft Corporation

FIGURE 2.33 Table of Contents Created with Links

a. Unpack the *one02p2Earnings.onepkg* data file in OneNote 2016 and rename it as **one02p2Earnings_LastFirst.**

b. Click the **Income Group section tab**. Click the **Earnings section tab**. Click **Password** in the Section group on the Review tab. Click **Set Password** in the Password Protection pane. In the Enter Password text box, type **OneNote2016**. Type **OneNote2016** in the Confirm Password text box and click **OK**. Close the Password Protection pane.

c. Click the **Navigate to parent section group arrow**. Click **File**, and click **Share**. Type **one02p2Earnings_LastFirst** in the Notebook Name box and click **Move Notebook**. Click **OK**. Click **Share with People**.

TROUBLESHOOTING: Your notebook will need to be on OneDrive to share it. If it is not on OneDrive, you will be presented with a screen to move the notebook. Type the notebook name in the file name box and click Move Notebook. If you are not signed in to your OneDrive account, you will need to sign in using your email address and password.

d. Type **your instructor's email address** in the *Type a name or email address to invite someone* box. Ensure Can edit is selected. In the message box, type **My notebook is one02p2Earnings_LastFirst**. Create a screenshot of the screen. Close the Share with People screen. Add a **Screenshots** section, and name the page **Screenshots**. Below the date, paste the screenshot of the Share with People screen. Sync and close the notebook.

e. Open *one02p2Earnings_LastFirst* in OneNote app. Click the **Show Navigation button** to the left of one02p2Earnings_LastFirst at the top of the screen. Click **Income** below one02p2Earnings_LastFirst in the Navigation Pane. The Earnings Section will display a message: *This section is password protected. Enter the password to unlock it.* Type **OneNote2016** in the Password text box, and press **Enter**.

TROUBLESHOOTING: If one02p2Earnings_LastFirst is not listed in the Notebook Pane, click More Notebooks. Scroll until the file name displays, and click the file name.

---

f. Navigate to the Earnings section 2nd QTR page. Click **Insert**, click **File**, and then select **Insert PDF Printout**. Navigate to data files, select *one02p2Income.pdf*, and click **Open**. Scroll up the notebook page to see the inserted file. Close the OneNote app.

g. Open one02p2Earnings_LastFirst in OneNote 2016. Click the **Blog section Article Ideas page tab**. Select the existing list of article ideas. Click **Bulleted List** on the Home tab. Click at the end of Sew a Sun Hat or Visor, and press **Enter**. Type **Sewing for Children** and press **Enter**. Type **Choosing the Right Needle** and press **Enter**. Type **Selecting the Right Fabric**.

h. Add a Section titled **Table of Contents**. Rename the page as **Table of Contents**. Click below the date on the page, and type **[[Approved Programs]]** and press **Enter**. Type **[[Applied Programs]]** and press **Enter**. Use the same method to add links to the following pages:

Future Articles

Screenshots

Earnings

Expenses

i. Verify the links work. Move the **Table of Contents section tab** to the right of the Navigation Pane arrow. Check the spelling in all sections.

j. Export the notebook as **one02p2Earnings_LastFirst.onepkg**. Close OneNote 2016.

k. Based on your instructor's directions submit one02p2Earnings_LastFirst.onepkg.

1 Create a Notebook for the Delta Iota Gamma Honor Society

FROM SCRATCH

Dr. Vamil Singh, the campus faculty sponsor of the Delta Iota Gamma Honor Society, asked you to create a OneNote notebook that will enable her to keep Honor Society members updated on current events and activities. Dr. Singh will provide View Only access to all members of the society so that they can see flyers on upcoming events, read meeting minutes, and learn about available scholarships. However, she needs the Scholarship Applicants page to be password protected.

a. Sign in to OneDrive. Create a notebook using OneNote Online. Click **+New**, and select **OneNote notebook**. Name the notebook **one02m1HonorSociety_LastFirst**. Add a new section if an Untitled Section is not available. Name the Untitled Section **Delta Iota Gamma**. Name the untitled page **Members**. Add a section titled **Scholarship Info**. Name the page **Scholarships**.

> **TROUBLESHOOTING:** Using Chrome browser? When you click Edit in OneNote, the External Protocol Request dialog box displays. Click Launch Application. When the Microsoft OneNote Security Notice dialog box displays, click Yes. When the Sign in dialog box displays, type your OneDrive email or phone number and click Next. Type your password in the Password box, and click Sign in. OneNote will sync the changes.
>
> You may also see a "Do you want to leave this site?" message. If so, click Yes.

b. Click **Edit in OneNote**. Insert the *one02m1SmallLogo.jpg* data file image on the Members page in the Delta Iota Gamma section in OneNote 2016. Insert a File Printout of the *one02m1Members.docx* data file.

c. Add a new page titled **Scholarship Applicants** to the Scholarship section. Change the page title on the Scholarships page to **Red, Darker 50%**, the font size to **36**, and the font to **Brush Script MT**. Double-click the **Format Painter** to copy the format to the titles on the Scholarship Applicants page and the Delta Iota Gamma section Members page. Click **Format Painter** to toggle it off.

d. Add a **Glasses Corner** page template from the Decorative template section to the Delta Iota Gamma section. Title the page **Meeting Agenda**. Insert a File Printout of *one02m1Agenda.docx* to the Meeting Agenda page.

e. Add a page and title it **Meeting Minutes**. On the Meeting Minutes page, insert a File Printout of *one02m1Minutes.docx*. Make the Meeting Agenda page a subpage to the Meeting Minutes. Use Format Painter to copy the page title format from the Members page to the Meeting Agenda and Meeting Minutes pages.

f. Display the Scholarship Applicants page, type **Students Applying for the Wilson B. Graham Honor Society Scholarship**, and then press **Enter**. Change the text to **Arial Black**, click in the font size box and type to change the font size to **11.5 pt**, and then change the font color to **Green, Darker 25%**.

g. Click below *Students Applying for the Wilson B. Graham Honor Society Scholarship*, and type the following information, pressing **Tab** after each item in the first column, and pressing **Enter** after each row except the last row:

Student	GPA
Susie Pace	3.90
Antonio Ruiz	3.89
Melody Luz	3.90
Ahn Min Joon	4.0
Tom Ayers	4.0
Bob Franklin	3.86

h. Click in the **first cell** (Student), click the **Table Tools Layout tab**, and then click **Insert Left** in the Insert group. Click in the first blank cell, and type **Application Received**. Widen the first column to display text on a single line. Select the **blank cells in the first column** and click **To Do Tag** in the Tags group on the Home tab.

i. Click the **To Do box** in front of Melody Luz's name.

j. Add a Section titled **Table of Contents**. Name the page **Table of Contents**. Use links to create a table of contents to all pages in all sections using your choice of method.

k. Password protect the Scholarship Applicants page using **OneNote2016** as the password. Remove the password, because this locks the entire Scholarship Info section. Add a section titled **Applicants**. Move the Scholarship Applicants page to the Applicants section. Delete the Untitled page in the Applicants section, and then using **OneNote2016** as the password, password protect the Applicants section.

l. Rearrange the order of the sections as **Table of Contents, Delta Iota Gamma, Scholarship Info**, and **Applicants**. Check spelling in all sections. Ignore Ahn Min Joon in the spelling check. **Synchronize** the notebook.

m. Export your notebook to your storage device as **one02m1HonorSociety_LastFirst.onepkg**.

n. Based on your instructor's directions, submit one02m1HonorSociety_LastFirst.onepkg.

2 Edit a Shared Notebook, Edit a Notebook in OneNote App

The Delta Iota Gamma Honor Society will be sending three students and Dr. Singh to the national convention in New Orleans. Dr. Singh asked you and your partner to locate three websites where airline tickets can be purchased. You will work with a classmate to complete these steps.

a. Unpack *one02m2Travel.onepkg* and rename the notebook as **one02m2Travel_LastFirst**. Move your notebook to OneDrive using the Share page on Backstage view. Share your notebook with your partner using the Share with People page on Backstage view. Type **I am sharing my one02m2Travel_LastFirst notebook with you.** Ensure Can edit is selected. Close OneNote.

b. Open your email. Open the email invitation to share your partner's notebook and click **View in OneDrive**. Close Outlook.

c. Log in to OneDrive. Click the **Edit Notebook arrow**, click **Edit in Microsoft OneNote**, and then click **Continue.** Click **Yes** twice.

d. Add a page titled **New Members Spring 2019** to the Delta Iota Gamma section and make the page a subpage below the **Members** page. Use Format Painter to change the title format to match the Members page. Type **New Members for Spring 2019** below the date, **bold** the text you just typed, and press **Enter** twice.

e. Type the following, pressing **Enter** after each name:

Your Name

Bradley Simmons

Lorena Gonzalez

DISCOVER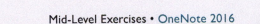
f. Close OneNote 2016. Verify your partner has completed steps a–e. Open OneNote 2016. Use the Notebook Navigation Pane to find and open *one02m2Travel_LastFirst*. Sync the file to get your partner's updates synced to your desktop notebook.

g. Click the **Recent Edits arrow** on the History tab and click **Last 30 Days**. Navigate to the **New Members Spring 2019 page**. Change Lorena Gonzalez to **Lorena Montez**. Close the Search Results pane.

h. Add a section titled **Prospects** and title the untitled page **Prospective Members**. Change the font on the page title to **Brush Script MT**, font size to **36**, and the font color to **Green, Darker 50%**. Press **Enter**.

DISCOVER
i. Insert the picture *one02m2Background.jpg*. Move the image until the top edge is even with the top of the page and the left edge is even with the first letter in the title. Right-click the **image** and click **Set Picture as Background**. Click the **View tab**. Click **Page Color** in the Page Setup group and select **Green**.

j. Type **The following individuals have been sent invitations:** below the image. Select the sentence and change the font to **Arial Black**, font size to **12**, and the font color to **Green, Darker 50%**. Press **Enter** twice.

k. Rename the page **Prospective Members November 2019**. Click below the sentence you previously typed and type the following names exactly as indicated below, pressing **Enter** after each:

Nancy Cordova

John Shackling

Jennifer Bell

Alexander Granxt

Select the four names you just typed and change the font color to **Black**, the font to **Arial**, and the font size to **14**.

l. Add a **Schedule meeting tag** from the Tags Gallery before each of the four names listed on the Prospective Members November 2019 page.

m. Add a link to the **New Members Spring 2019 page** and the **Prospective Members November 2019 page** to the Table of Contents. For all sections, check spelling, and correct errors.

n. Create a new section titled **Travel Plans**. Title the untitled page **Tickets** and press **Enter**. Using the Research tool on the Review tab, locate three websites that offer airline tickets. Copy each of the three URLs and paste them in the Tickets page, pressing **Enter** after pasting each. Apply a **bullet list** to the URLs. Close the Research pane. Close your browser.

o. Navigate to the Prospects section tab. Use Find Tags in the Tags group of the Home tab to find the Schedule meeting tags.

p. Click **Create Summary Page** and rename the page **Tags Summary**. Close the Tags Summary pane.

q. Add links to the Table of Contents for the **Tickets page** and the **Tags Summary page**.

r. Apply the page title format from the Members page in the Delta Iota Gamma section to the **Tags Summary** and **Tickets** pages.

s. Sync the notebook. Export the complete notebook to your storage media as **one02m2Travel_LastFirst.onepkg**. Close OneNote 2016. Close OneNote Online and log out of OneDrive.

t. Based on your instructor's directions, submit one02m2Travel_LastFirst.onepkg.

Beyond the Classroom

OneNote Presentation

GENERAL CASE

Create a presentation for incoming freshmen on how using OneNote helps you keep up with course work and helps in preparation for exams. The presentation requirements are:

- Name the presentation **one02b1Presentation_LastFirst.pptx**.
- A cover slide with an appropriate title with your name in the subtitle.
- An introductory slide that explains what the presentation will cover.
- A minimum of six slides of content.
- At least two appropriate images of your choice (these can be screenshots).
- A summary slide.
- A works-cited slide with all images, including screenshots.

Based on your instructor's directions, submit one02b1Presentation_LastFirst.

Preventing Data Loss

DISASTER RECOVERY

Many students have lost important papers or research notes because they did not have a backup, and either lost their storage device or the device was damaged or malfunctioned. Microsoft OneNote works with a variety of apps for your phone, tablet, or PC, some of which would be helpful in preventing data loss. Visit **http://www.onenote.com/apps**. Review the apps Microsoft recommends. Write a one- or two-page paper discussing the following:

- Select three apps you think might be useful for students to use with OneNote to prevent data loss. Explain why you chose these three particular apps.
- Which other apps would you be interested in using? Explain why.
- Would any of these apps be more effective than simply exporting a copy of the notebook to a different storage location or syncing the notebook to OneDrive? Explain your answer.

Save your document as **one02b2Apps_LastFirst.docx**. Make sure your name and the current date are on the first two lines at the top of the first page. Based on your instructor's directions, submit one02b2Apps_LastFirst.

Capstone Exercise

Server Side Team Notebook

As a student intern for Search It, Inc., you have been asked to add content to an existing OneNote notebook for the Server Side Programming Team. The notebook contains sections and pages to provide information and announcements to the team.

> **TROUBLESHOOTING: PARTNER NEEDED**
>
> To complete this exercise, you will need a partner. If your instructor does not assign partners, select a partner to work with for this exercise.

Add a Template and Password Protect the Section

You will add a template to a new Manager section and password protect the section.

a. Unpack *one02c1ServerSide.onepkg* and rename it as **one02c1ServerSide_LastFirst**. Move the notebook to OneDrive.

b. Add a section named Management. Insert the **Binoculars Corner** template page from the Decorative category. Rename the template page **Management Training**. Close the Templates pane. Delete any untitled page.

c. Insert a file printout of the *one02c1Flyer.docx* data file on the Management Training page. Because the entire team will have access to the notebook, the Management section needs to be password protected. Password protect the Management section using **OneNote2016** as the password. Close the Password Protection pane.

Work with Partner to Add Content

You will share your notebook with your partner and instructor, add Team Activities content, and format the content.

a. Sync and share the notebook with your partner. Close the notebook. Navigate to OneDrive. Open your partner's *one02c1ServerSide_PartnerName* notebook, where PartnerName is replaced by your partner's last name and first name. Click **Sign In** in the top right corner, click **Edit in OneNote**, and then click **Edit in Microsoft OneNote**.

b. Add a page and name it **Team Activities** to the Activities section. Type **Print the attached file, fill in your preferences, and give the completed survey to the team administrative assistant by Tuesday.** Press **Enter** twice. Attach the *one02c1Survey.docx* data file.

c. Select the text you typed in step c. Bold the text. Change the font color to **Green, Darker 25%**, the font size to **14**, and the font to **Arial Black**.

d. Sync and close your partner's notebook.

Add Content and Tags

You will add content to the Team Activities page, type a list of team members, add To Do Tags.

a. Open your one02c1ServerSide_LastFirst notebook with OneNote 2016 and sync the notebook. Insert spreadsheet *one02c1Results.xlsx* as an Existing Excel Spreadsheet below the previous content on the Team Activities page. Click below the Inserted spreadsheet, press **Enter**, and type **We will have a potluck at our manager's house for our monthly team outing. If you can make it, please check your name.** Press **Enter** twice.

b. Type the following, pressing **Enter** after each name.

Student Name
Carla Powell
Juan Rodriguez
Abe Goldstein
Jamil Jefferson

c. Select the typed list of names. Click **To Do Tag** in the Tags group on the Home tab. Click the **To Do boxes** to the left of Student FirstLast and Jamil Jefferson.

d. Display the Activities section Company Activities page, and select the page title. Change the font to **Brush Script MT**. Change the font size to **36 pt**. Change the font color to **Green, Darker 50%**.

e. Sync and close one02c1ServerSide_LastFirst.

Add Pages, Research Sites, Create a Table of Contents, and Use Format Painter

Using OneNote Online, you will add a page titled JavaScript to the Notes section, and add and format a list of URLs to be used as reference sites. You will also research an additional site, format the bullet list, add a table of contents, and use Format Painter to format all page titles.

a. Log into OneDrive. Open OneNote Online. Navigate to the Announcements section Team Shirts subpage. Change the font of the header text in the first row of the table to **Verdana**.

b. Add a page to the Notes section, title it **JavaScript**, and then press **Enter**.

c. Type **Use these reference sites for JavaScript coding questions:** below the date, and press **Enter** twice. Using a bullet list, type the following, pressing **Enter** after each URL:

www.w3schools.com/js/default.asp

www.javascriptsource.com/tutorials

d. Click **Edit in OneNote.** Use the Research tool on the Review tab to locate a third site to use as a reference for JavaScript coding questions. Copy the URL and paste it on the line below www.javascriptsource.com/tutorials.

e. Select the **bullet list**, and change the font to **Arial.**

f. Add a section titled **Contents.** Rename the Untitled page as **Table of Contents.** Create a table of contents of the five sections in the main notebook using the method of your choice. Add links to the CSP Team and Mainframe Team section groups using the method of your choice. Move the Contents section tab just right of the Notebook pane.

g. Use the Format Painter to format all page titles in all sections the same as the Activities Company Activities page except the pages in the section groups. Sync the notebook. View the JavaScript page in your notebook to verify the sync.

h. Export **one02c1ServerSide_LastFirst** to your storage device. Close OneNote 2016. Close OneDrive. Based on your instructor's directions, submit one02c1ServerSide_LastFirst.onepkg.

Glossary

Collaboration Two or more groups or individuals working together on a common goal.

Clipboard A section of computer memory set aside to hold temporary items.

Container An area on a page that is used to hold text, images, or other content.

Export A method to save the entire notebook, a page, a group, or a section to a different location.

Fair Use A provision of copyright law that allows limited copying for commenting, criticizing, or supporting a statement.

Find Tags A command that makes it easy to find marked content in a notebook.

Format Painter A tool that enables users to copy the formatting of one selection and paste it to another section

Merge The technique used to combine the contents of two or more pages, sections, or notebooks.

Notebook A file created by OneNote to hold content divided into sections and pages.

Notebook Pane A pane that provides access to other open OneNote notebooks, add a notebook, or open notebooks not listed.

OneDrive A free online storage platform that also provides users with access to limited versions of some web-based Microsoft Office applications.

OneNote 2016 Microsoft's most recent version of OneNote, which is note-taking software designed specifically for the laptop and desktop computer.

OneNote app The version of OneNote created primarily for touch screen tablets and smartphones.

OneNote Online Microsoft's OneDrive version of the OneNote application.

Online app A limited function application that is available on the OneDrive platform.

Optical character recognition (OCR) Software that converts text in scanned documents and photographs into text.

Page The content area inside OneNote sections.

Page Pane The section of the OneNote 2016 screen which displays page tabs.

Page tab A tab in the Page Pane that provides navigation between section pages.

Page template A predesigned format used for OneNote pages.

Pass phrase A group of words used as a password, or as the base for a password made up of the initials of the words.

Password protection A tool that prevents unauthorized individuals seeing, adding, or deleting content of a section.

Path The exact route a computer uses to locate a file.

Plagiarism The use of another's ideas or creative work without crediting the owner of the idea or work.

Quick Access Toolbar A mini toolbar that contains three command buttons: Back, Undo, and Customize. A fourth command, Touch/Mouse Mode, may display on touch-screen devices.

Ribbon A graphical user interface across the top of the screen that contains tabs separating types of commands by function.

Screenshot An image created from the content displayed on your monitor.

Search box A tool that enables users to locate specific information or specific types of information in a notebook, section, or page.

Search scope Settings that determine where OneNote looks when searching for information users need to find.

Search term A phrase or keyword relevant to the content users are trying to find.

Section The primary division in a notebook, each of which may contain one page or many pages.

Section tab The primary division in a notebook, each of which may contain one page or many pages.

Section group A specialized tab that gives you the option to organize sections into related groupings.

Share A feature that enables users to give access to their notebooks to other individuals.

Snipping Tool A tool included in Windows 7, Windows 8, and Windows 10 accessory applications that is designed to capture screenshots.

Subpage A page that is denoted by indention below a previous page, used to add additional information to a specific page topic.

Sync An action that saves an exact duplicate of changes made in OneNote 2016, OneNote Online, and OneNote app, so that all versions of the application have access to the same information.

Tag An electronic marker inserted into a page to mark specific types of content.

Templates pane A pane that contains a selection of pre-designed and formatted pages that can be inserted into a section.

Toggle command A command switch that is either on or off.

Wiki A shared electronic database or file with content that can be changed, added to, or deleted by anyone with whom it has been shared.

Index